Philip Henry Sheridan, James F. (James Fingal) Gregory, W. H. (William Henry) Forwood, Sanford C. (Sanford Cobb) Kellogg

Report of Lieut. General P.H. Sheridan, dated September 20, 1881

Of his Expedition through the Big Horn Mountains, Yellowstone National Park, etc.

Philip Henry Sheridan, James F. (James Fingal) Gregory, W. H. (William Henry) Forwood, Sanford C. (Sanford Cobb) Kellogg

Report of Lieut. General P.H. Sheridan, dated September 20, 1881
Of his Expedition through the Big Horn Mountains, Yellowstone National Park, etc.

ISBN/EAN: 9783337216580

Printed in Europe, USA, Canada, Australia, Japan

Cover: Foto ©ninafisch / pixelio.de

More available books at **www.hansebooks.com**

REPORT

OF

LIEUT. GENERAL P. H. SHERIDAN,

DATED

SEPTEMBER 20, 1881,

OF HIS EXPEDITION THROUGH THE

BIG HORN MOUNTAINS, YELLOWSTONE NATIONAL PARK, ETC.,

TOGETHER WITH REPORTS OF

LIEUT. COL. J. F. GREGORY, A. D. C.,
SURGEON W. H. FORWOOD, AND
CAPT. S. C. KELLOGG, FIFTH CAVALRY.

———

Official copy:

R. C. DRUM,
Adjutant-General.

ADJUTANT-GENERAL'S OFFICE,
December 13, 1831.

———•◆•———

WASHINGTON:
GOVERNMENT PRINTING OFFICE.
1882.

EXPEDITION THROUGH THE BIG HORN MOUNTAINS, YELLOWSTONE PARK, ETC.

REPORT OF LIEUTENANT-GENERAL P. H. SHERIDAN.

HEADQUARTERS MILITARY DIVISION OF THE MISSOURI,
Chicago, Ill., September 20, 1881.

GENERAL: For the purpose of acquiring additional knowledge of the interesting country in and about the Big Horn Mountains, and the valleys of the Big Horn, Grey Bull, and Stinking Water, and Clark's Fork, lying west of and between the Big Horn and the main chain of the Rocky Mountains, and thence crossing the main chain to the National Park, I started on July 27, accompanied by General Delos B. Sacket, Inspector-General, U. S. A., Lieut. Cols. M. V. Sheridan, and James F. Gregory, of my staff; General M. D. Hardin, retired; General William E. Strong, Mr. Samuel Johnson and Mr. E. N. Sheldon, of Chicago; and Dr. W. P. Wesselhoft and son, of Boston, and proceeded by the Union Pacific Railroad to Rock Creek Station, and from thence due north by land transportation to Fort Fetterman, distant 85 miles from Rock Creek Station. This journey from the railroad was made in one day. The country traveled over was, for the most part, uninteresting, except at a few points, until Fort Fetterman was reached, just before sundown, July 30. Although the country was unsettled, large herds of cattle, for some distance from the railroad and about Fort Fetterman, indicated the presence of numerous cattle ranches.

Resting at Fetterman the night of July 30, at an early hour next morning we started for Powder River, traveling in a general direction nearly northwest, crossing the south and north forks of the Belle Fourche, which river, with the South Fork of the Cheyenne, almost encircles the Black Hills, reaching Powder River before sunset, July 31, distant from Fetterman 90 miles.

The country traveled over was rolling, and to some extent sandy, with abundance of sage brush, sparsely watered, but, strange to say, was occupied by some of the largest herds of cattle in Wyoming, and the ranges were considered excellent. South of the line traveled this day, all the way down to the Union Pacific Railroad, large herds of cattle and comfortable cattle ranches are to be found.

Powder River Valley, where we rested for the night, is not prepossessing, especially about the crossing, but up and down the river, from this point, it offers to the cattleman pastures of great value, and is occupied by thousands of cattle. We stopped near the post of old Fort Reno, abandoned long ago. All that is necessary in this valley for cultivation, with satisfactory results, is industry and irrigation, for which latter the river offers good inducements as there is sufficient water.

The next morning, August 1, we made an early start, and almost from the moment we left the valley of the Powder River, traveling northwestward, we discovered an improvement in the soil and grasses. At about 12 m. we reached Fort McKinney, named after an officer killed in an engagement which Colonel Mackenzie had with the Northern Cheyennes, not very distant from this military post.

McKinney is truly, in location and surroundings, a beautiful post. It is on Clear Fork of Powder River, with good, fine granite soil under foot. The quarters for officers and men are fairly comfortable, but wanting in repairs and other improvements in detail. Ditches conveying pure, clear water encircle the parade ground, in front of the quarters of the officers and men, and empty out into an extensive garden, on a lower plateau, just below and behind the post.

Early on the morning of August 2 we resumed our march through the undulating country lying between the base of the Big Horn Mountains and Wolf Mountains—a much lower range farther to the north and east—reaching Tongue River, distant 55 miles, about two o'clock in the afternoon.

The country between Clear Fork, Fort McKinney, and Tongue River is excellent in soil, and, for natural nutritious grasses, the best I have ever seen, with the exception, perhaps, of the pastures of the higher ranges of the Big Horn Mountains and like ranges on the main chain of the Rocky Mountains, along Clark's Fork, where the grazing can only be for the summer months.

Between McKinney and Tongue River there are numerous streams, the valleys of which are being settled up by thrifty farmers, with extensive fields of wheat, oats, and barley. The vegetable gardens were excellent, the varieties embracing most of those raised in eastern sections of our country. The fields of wheat, oats, and barley were of better quality and greater in quantity, to the acre, than those seen on the east side of the Missouri.

The streams coming down from the Big Horn Mountains, and emptying into the Clear Fork of Powder River and Tongue River, are numerous, the grasses strong and nutritious—bunch grass preponderating. The same character of country continues on northward across the Little Horn and Greasy Grass Creeks, with even an improvement of the soil and a greater variety of grasses, all the way to the Big Horn River, distant about 75 miles.

At a distance of 15 or 20 miles north of Tongue River, in the direction of old Fort C. F. Smith, the eastern line of the reservation of the Crows is reached, and no settlement of this valuable country has been permitted. The Crows have never occupied it heretofore, and never could hold it until the Northern Cheyennes, Sioux, and Arapahoes were driven out by the war of 1876. This country now forms part of the Crow Reservation, which contains about *six and a quarter millions* of acres, and as the whole number of Crows does not exceed 3,500, this gives each man, woman, and child in the tribe about 2,000 acres. The greater portion of it should be purchased from them by the government, for what it is *worth to them*, and opened to settlement, and but a short time would elapse until it would be densely covered by thrifty farmers and by thousands and thousands of cattle.

In former times, the country between the Yellowstone Valley and the base of the Big Horn Mountains was the winter range of the great northern herd of buffalo. They are now being killed off and replaced by a better and more useful animal—the cattle of civilization.

That portion of this valuable country claimed and acknowledged by the government as belonging to the Crow Nation, never did belong to hem by conquest or occupation, so far as is known. It was held by the Northern Cheyennes and their allies, the Sioux and Arapahoes, and occupied by these people for a long period. After the military, in 1876, drove out these tribes, who held it at least by right of conquest, and certainly by that of possession, the Crows came in to spread their blankets on their soil, as they said, and gather berries and roots for a month or two in the summer. It is too valuable to remain idle for such insignificant productions.

The country between the eastern base of the Big Horn Range and the Wolf and Rosebud Mountains, and down to the Yellowstone River, is from about 90 to 150 miles in width and 180 in length; if it had added to it that portion of the Crow Reservation between the Little Big Horn and the Big Horn Rivers, it would have an encouraging future. The streams which run from the mountains into the Clear Fork, Tongue River, and Little Horn are clear and rapid, and the valleys are broad. The soil is good, except in the broken Bad Lands down towards the Yellowstone, and is fully as susceptible of cultivation as other settled lands this side of the Missouri, and in my judgment will produce, independent of irrigation, after two or three plowings. The pasturage is the best, for the year round, of any section of the United States. There is no record of very bad winter snows, last winter being the worst ever known. There are no heavy or continuous rains in the late summer and fall, and the grass makes good, dry hay on the stalk, instead of falling to the ground and rotting, as is the case in the east and south. When I visited this country, less than four years ago, it was the land of the Indian and the buffalo; now it has numerous farms and cattle ranches, with cattle by the thousands, this side of the Little Horn.

At 6 a. m., August 4, we moved from the banks of Tongue River and ascended the grassy, precipitous slope of the Big Horn Mountains, north of Tongue River, making a steep ascent to the first elevated ridge, which commanded a view to the north and eastward, well on to the valley of the Yellowstone River. We continued for the day gradually ascending, in a direction parallel with Tongue River, and passing through a succession of grassy parks encircled by pine timber, until we reached a point near the junction of the north and south forks, where we encamped. Next day we resumed our march, following up the North Fork through beautiful natural parks, larger and more interesting than on the day previous; in fact, they were almost as complete in beauty as those cultivated by the hand and skill of man. Passing over the main divide, nearly 10,000 feet in altitude, we made camp in a beautiful resting place for the night. From this camp we could look over to the west and see an extensive country, in which runs the Wind River—with the Grey Bull and Stinking Water Rivers in the distance—and far beyond these rivers, and from whence they take their source, we could see the main line of the Rocky Mountains. There are few places, if any, where a grander or more interesting view can be had.

During our succeeding marches from this camp, we crossed innumerable streams of pure, cold water, most of them having their source in large flowing springs. Next day we continued our march towards old Fort C. F. Smith, and well along the summit of the mountains, through parks similar to those mentioned, tufted with a luxuriant growth of bunch and gama grasses. On the succeeding day, in the line of marching, we again came down the mountain on the edge of the Black Cañon, and from the overhanging bank we looked down to its parky meadow bottom, 2,900 feet below—a rare and interesting picture that it is hoped will be placed on canvas by the highest order of talent at some future day.

On August 8 we reached the old abandoned military post of Fort C. F. Smith, and encamped on the banks of the Big Horn. Here we found the Big Horn too deep to ford, but the commanding officer at Fort Custer, 40 miles below, had, in accordance with instructions sent him, a company of cavalry and two boats to ferry us across. The animals were driven into the stream and swam over.

On the morning of August 10, at six, we resumed our march and crossed over a grassy country, making for Pryor's Gap. We encamped on Sage Creek.

Next day we resumed the march, encamping for the night on Pryor's Fork of the Yellowstone, a bold running stream filled with large trout, from which the command took several hundred, varying in size from 1½ to 2½ pounds. The valley of Pryor's River is broad, with fine alluvial soil. Just below on the river, distant 4 or 5 miles, was an encampment of 70 or 80 lodges of Crow Indians, the first of this tribe we had seen, except our guides, although, while in the Big Horn Mountains, we passed near by a large camp who were there for a short time gathering berries.

In the last two days we had crossed the Big Horn Valley, rather narrow at our line of march, but widening out further down towards the Yellowstone. From where we crossed this valley, to the Yellowstone, it is about 75 miles in length and from 10 to 15 miles broad. It has excellent soil and good grasses for grazing purposes. The country from this over to Pryor's Fork is higher, with several streams coming down from Pryor's Mountains, and is unequaled for grazing purposes, from the good grasses and from the freedom from snow in the winter. It is subjected in the winter to warm winds, called out there the "Chanook" winds, which cause the snow to melt and be absorbed rapidly.

On August 12 we resumed the march, passing Pryor's Gap, a low and easy passage-way, with a picturesque and abrupt mountain on either side. This gap had been the scene of a contest between the Crow Indians on one side and the Northern Cheyennes and Sioux on the other, several years ago, in which, according to the testimony of our Crow guide, their side had been successful. Numerous piles of stones, conical in shape, some large and some small, marked the resting places of those killed in this engagement. Each of our guides deposited, according to the custom of their people, tobacco, pipes, coin, or some articles taken from their persons, as offerings to their companions whose bones rested under these heaps of stones.

We made a very long march this day, crossing Sage Creek and a level plain somewhat covered with sage brush, until we reached Bridger's road, and thence through a remarkably bad section of Bad Lands until we encamped on Clark's Fork of the Yellowstone for the night. Next day we resumed our march up Clark's Fork, skirted by Bad Lands on the left and a high, broken, grassy, rolling country across Clark's Fork on the right. Down Clark's Fork towards the Yellowstone, as far as we could see, the valley looked well, but on the line of our march up the stream, while the soil was good, irrigation will be necessary to get good results, in grasses or from cultivation. It resembles the soil of the Salt Lake Valley, before Mormon industry and irrigation had made it, as it now is, so fertile and bountiful.

The direction we wished to take up Clark's Fork had to be abandoned, as it required us to cross the river many times, and the water was too high for fording. We therefore made a new trail by keeping on the west side of the river, occasionally being forced by bluffy banks to pass out into the Bad Lands, to round a point. This river offers, from the rapidity of the current and its generally low banks, the best facilities for irrigation, at small expense, that I have seen anywhere.

On August 14 we reached the base of the main chain of the Rocky Mountains, not far from the mouth of Clark's Fork Cañon.

At six, on the morning of August 15, we commenced the ascent of the main chain of the Rocky Mountains, at this point called Clark's Fork Mountain, and not far distant from the mouth of the cañon of Clark's Fork River. This cañon ranks in length and in grandeur of scenery with the cañons of the Yellowstone, the Arkansas, the Animas, and the Colorado; it is 24 miles in length, and at places nearly 3,000 feet in depth. We passed up the mountain range, sometimes on foot and sometimes on horseback, until we reached the summit ridge, and, turning along the ridge through a succession of grassy parks, inclosed with beautiful varieties of pine and cedar, we reached a point commanding a view of surprising magnificence. To the east the summit of the Big Horn Range was in view, distant over 100 miles, while intermediate was the smaller range of Pryor's Mountains. To the south were the valleys of Wind River, Grey Bull, and Stinking Water, and, encircling these valleys, farther to the southwest, were the Shoshone and Wind River Ranges, with their lines of perpetual snow, extending around to old Camp Stambaugh. In the valley of Stinking River were the isolated peaks of Hart and Cedar Mountains, and bearing more to the northwest were the high peaks of the Stinking River Mountains, the snow range, and Bear Tooth Mountains, while up the valley of Clark's Fork and near where it takes its rise, standing up against the sky, were Pilot Knob, and Index Peak, the great landmarks of the Rocky Mountains. After feasting our eyes on this view, unparalleled in grandeur and extent, we continued our march through grassy parks until we reached the edge of the valley of Indian Creek, which was to be our camp for the night. We made the descent of 1,900 feet into the valley, in a distance less than a mile. Horse and man did considerable sliding in getting down this precipitous descent. Indian Creek empties into Clark's Fork, and our camp was in a beautiful spot not far from its mouth.

Next morning, at six, we resumed our march, following up Clark's Fork to Crandle's Creek, encamping in its valley, and not far distant from the main river. Here game was very abundant. However, no distinction in this respect should be made, for elk, deer, antelope, mountain sheep, bear, mountain grouse Richardson grouse, sage chickens, and trout were abundant on the whole line of our march from Tongue River.

As it was necessary to give a day's rest for the repair of pack-saddles and readjustment of packs, word was sent round that we would remain in this beautiful camp for the next day. A party was at once organized, consisting of Colonel Sheridan, General Strong, Mr. Sheldon, with Campbell, the guide, and Patrick, one of the head packers, to go over to the frozen lakes near the foot of Bear Tooth Range, and take an evening's hunt for elk. The distance was about 10 miles. They killed, in the evening, seven elk, and could have killed many more, as the country was occupied by hundreds of these beautiful animals. One herd of 150 amused them by swimming with their young in the lake, taking, as it were, an evening bath. The party did not kill any more, as the orders were that no more game should be killed than could be consumed by the command. The elk killed were very fat, and of fine flavor. Previous to this time we had killed twelve or thirteen along the route of our daily marches, which, with the other game we killed in the same way, kept our large command bountifully supplied with fresh meat.

On August 18, at six, we resumed our march up Clark's Fork, the trail being much rougher than on any day previous, and encamped at the base of Pilot Knob and Index Peak.

Next morning, at six, we resumed our march, passing along the base of Pilot Knob and Index Peak, and, turning the latter to the northward we crossed over the summit of the mountains, and encamped on Soda Butte Creek, a tributary of the Upper Yellowstone.

Just after crossing the divide, we struck a mining camp, where we found a few miners with, I think, good claims. They were there watching their claims, but could not work them, as they were, unfortunately, on the Crow Reservation, but just on the edge of it. Two or three of these men had been there for eight or nine years, waiting for some Congressional action to permit them to make their fortunes. If such relief should come I believe they will do well, as they have good "prospects," and there are plenty more of the same kind in the neighborhood. It would be well if Congress could give relief to these poor fellows. Some of them, at least, located without knowing that they were on the Crow Reservation; subsequently, the Crows wanted to give up all their present reservation, and to go over to the Judith Basin, and there were, for a long time, doubts as to what were the limits of the reservation, or where it would be. This mining country is of no use to the Crows, and should be purchased by the government at a nominal price, and should be thrown open to add to our gold and silver production.

At the usual hour in the morning of August 20 we resumed our journey down Soda Butte Creek, passing by an extinct geyser, and about eight o'clock reached and crossed the east branch of the Yellowstone River, thence proceeding down the valley of this stream until near its junction with the main river, when we crossed over on Baronette's Bridge, making our camp on the west side. While coming down the valley of Soda Butte Creek we had crossed the line and entered the Yellowstone Park. Early next morning we resumed our march via Tower Falls and Mount Washburn; thence up the cañon of the Yellowstone, encamping at the great falls.

On the morning of August 22 we resumed the march, passing by Sulphur Mountain, the Devil's Caldron, Mud Geysers, where we made an early camp, most of our party going up to the Yellowstone Lake, but a few miles distant. Next morning, at the usual hour, we resumed our march, passing through large open parks, alternating with dense pine woods, and one or two low, swampy bottoms, making by our day's journey the Lower Geyser Basin, encamping very near the Fountain Geyser, and the crater of the Paint Pots. Next day we continued our journey, crossing the Lower Geyser Basin, and up the valley of the Fire Hole River to the Upper Geyser Basin, pitching our camp only a few hundred yards from the geyser known as Old Faithful. From this camp we had the pleasure of witnessing, during our stay, the action of nearly all the grand geysers of this wonderful place, so fully described by Barlow, Hayden, and others. The phenomena witnessed was fully up to and exceeded our expectations. Our only regret is the indifference shown by the government, probably from want of appreciation of the wonders of this interesting country. The area of the park is 3,300 square miles; the altitude is high; the surface is covered by open grassy parks, surrounded by dense pine forests, and having near its center the Yellowstone Cañon, and the Upper, Lower, and Middle Geyser Basins. We found the forests on fire for miles, at five or six different places. The craters of many of the geysers, where the water was spouted up as high as 200 feet in column, were partly wedged up by good sized trees pushed in with the butt end down, so that our large force of men could not pull them out, and visitors, men, women, and children, with axes, hatchets, and hammers, were there then, mutilating the craters of the geysers in the most wanton and provoking manner.

The Congressional appropriation of $15,000 annually for this park out of which comes the salary of the superintendent and game-keeper, and perhaps some incidental expenses, is too small to give much of a balance for the improvement of the roads and trails, so that really the work done in the summer has to be so temporary that it is washed out by the winter rains. These two men cannot take care of this extensive park. A larger appropriation should be given by Congress, and an engineer officer should be detailed to expend it on improvement of the trails and roads, with a company or two of calvary to be stationed in the park for the summer, to watch and prevent the burning of forests, and the mutilation of the craters and other singular phenomena of the geysers.

On August 27 we took up the line of march down the Fire Hole River, encamping at the foot of the Lower Geyser Basin, and next day crossed over to the Madison, thence up that river, leaving it at the foot of Tyhee Pass, through which our direction led over to Henry Lake, and thence down Henry's Fork of Snake River, and over to Camas Station, on the Utah Northern Railroad, where we took cars for Ogden, and thence by the Union Pacific Railroad for home.

The Tyhee Pass at Henry Lake is very low. One can scarcely realize that he is passing through one of the gaps of the Rocky Mountains. A railroad could be constructed from Williams Junction, on the Utah Northern Division of the Union Pacific Railroad, or from several other points not far distant, by Henry Lake and Tyhee Pass down the Madison and through the short cañon of Gibbon's Fork, and up the Fire Hole River to the Upper Geyser Basin, on almost a minimum grade.

At Camas Station we separated from our escort, which was directed to return to Fort Laramie, via the Teton and Union Passes, to the head waters of Wind River, thence down that river to Fort Washakie, on the Shoshone Reservation, and thence home by the nearest and most practicable route.

Our troops had never gone through this pass, and but little was known of the route except to the Shoshone Indians. I submit the very interesting report of Colonel Kellogg, whose company formed our escort, descriptive of this route. I also submit the exceedingly interesting report of Surgeon W. H. Forwood on the flora of the country passed over on our long but exceedingly interesting expedition. We had no sickness, no accidents, and our escort and pack trains were returned to Fort Laramie in good condition, after having traveled some 1,609 miles. A map of the Yellowstone National Park, Big Horn Mountains, and adjacent country, prepared in the office of the Chief Engineer of this Division, is trnsmitted herewith.

I have the honor to be, general, very respectfully, your obedient servant,

P. H. SHERIDAN,
Lieutenant-General, Commanding.

Brig-Gen. R. C. DRUM,
Adjutant-General U. S. A., Washington, D. C.

/

REPORT OF LIEUT. COL. JAMES F. GREGORY.

CHICAGO, ILL.. *October* 20, 1881.

GENERAL : I have the honor to submit the accompanying journal of the trip made by yourself and party the past season through the Big Horn Mountains, Yellowstone National Park, &c.

I have not dwelt upon the wonders of the park, because they have been described so many times in the journals of the country as well as in official reports. A section of the map of Yellowstone National Park, Big Horn Mountains, and adjacent territory, with our trail delineated thereon, accompanies this communication.

Very respectfully, your obedient srevant,

JAMES F. GREGORY,
Lieutenant-Colonel and Aide-de-Camp.

Lieutenant-General P. H. SHERIDAN,
United States Army, Chicago, Ill.

JOURNAL.

In conformity with instructions from the Lieutenant-General, I left Chicago with camp equipage and supplies on the 15th of July, to establish a camp for the party on Tongue River, and have everything in readiness for the mountain trip when the General and his party should arrive there, as was contemplated, about the 2d of August. The escort and pack trains had been ordered from headquarters to report to me at Fort McKinney; and a non-commissioned officer and four enlisted men from Fort Fetterman, with two army wagons and one spring wagon as transportation, to report to me upon my arrival at Rock Creek, on the Union Pacific Railroad, on the evening of the 17th of July.

We left Rock Creek on the 18th, arriving at Fort Fetterman on the 20th, and at Fort McKinney on the 26th. At the latter post we remained two days, preparing our *impedimenta* for packing and receiving additional forage and supplies.

Bvt. Lieut. Col. S. C. Kellogg, captain Fifth Cavalry, with his company, I, of that regiment, and Mr. Thomas Moore, chief packer of the Department of the Platte, with four pack trains, reported to me for duty at Fort McKinney. We started for Tongue River on the 29th and arrived there on the 31st of July.

The march from the railroad was as pleasant as could have been expected in passing over so desolate a country as that between the Laramie Hills and the Clear Fork of the Powder River.

The days were extremely hot, the thermometer in the shade standing between 90° and 100° F. at 2 p. m., twice reaching the latter point; the nights, however, were all cool and pleasant. Antelopes were seen nearly every day on the trip, and two were killed; sage chickens and doves more abundant, and furnished our mess with an agreeable change of diet. The young sage chickens are delicious eating, their meat much resembling that of the dusky grouse; after they are half grown the meat has acquired a sagey and bitter taste, and is no temptation to the palate when other food is to be had. The country was very dry and dusty from the Platte River to Clear Fork; grass very poor; water scarce and alkaline, so that it was a delightful change to arrive on the banks of the deliciously cool water, Clear Fork.

I may mention, as a curious entomological fact, that I killed a scorpion in my bed during the night we camped at the crossing of the Powder

River. It was about 2 inches long, and of a lighter color than the Texas variety.

I had never before heard of the existence of scorpions so far north, but the telegraph operator at Powder River informed me that he had frequently heard of their being found there. Rattlesnakes were killed nearly every day of our trip after leaving Fort Fetterman, and at Tongue River eight were killed around Colonel Kellogg's tent. Our camp on the Piney was at the old crossing, just above the site of old Fort Phil Kearney. No trace now remains of the old post; a ranchman cultivates a large portion of the bottom near its former site. Wood, good water, and grass are abundant; and in gazing upon the beautiful and peaceful scene one almost fails to conceive the fact that only fifteen years ago this was the far-distant outpost of civilization. Indians swarmed over the country, and, just over the hill in front of us, in 1866, Fetterman and his command were massacred by the Sioux under Red Cloud within full hearing of the post; whilst the agonized remnant of the garrison within the walls, knowing that a fight was in progress but unable to help, hoped and prayed for husbands, brothers, and friends until all hope was extinguished. Now, not only the Piney but all of the streams flowing from the Big Horn Mountains to the eastward are dotted with the buildings and fields of the farmer and ranchman, whilst the cattle that cover the hills appear almost numberless.

There are no trout in any of the streams which are tributary to the Powder River, whilst they abound in all the tributaries of the Tongue River. Clear Fork seems to be as fine a stream for trout as one might find in a lifetime, but there are none in it. Whilst in camp on the Tongue River the soldiers and packers occupied their leisure in fishing, and I have no doubt caught nearly a thousand pounds in the three days we were there. The trout were of all sizes, up to about 3 pounds.

On the 31st of July J. A. Campbell, scout from Fort Custer, with five Crow Indians and one squaw, who were to accompany us on the trip, arrived in camp. The Indians had come by way of the Crow camp on Pryor's Creek, and report that the Crow camp, of about thirty teepees, had been burned out, and were oblighed "to hustle" to save their prop' erty from destruction.

On the 1st of August a man came from Campbell and Hardin's ranch, about 10 miles below us, on the Tongue River, and reported that all of the cattlemen in the country had been fighting prairie fire for two days and nights, and had succeeded in stopping it at Tongue River. Campbell said that two years ago the whole country was burned from the Madison to the Powder River, which was a great disaster to the cattle interest, and a similar one was feared now. The fires burned brightly at night during our stay on Tongue River, and caused us some uneasiness, but we were not disturbed. Afterwards, from the heights of the mountains, we could see a large area of burnt district to the north and northeast of us.

On the 2d of August General Sheridan and party arrived in camp, having traveled from Rock Creek in spring wagons, with relays at various points along the road. Traveling only by day, they made the distance from Rock Creek to camp on Tongue River, 288 miles, in four days, their longest drive in one day being 90 miles. On the evening of the same day Dr. Wm. Wesselhoeft and son, of Boston, who had been invited by General Sheridan to accompany him on the trip, arrived by special stage from Rock Creek.

The party, as organized at Tongue River, consisted of the following persons and animals:

Lieutenant-General P. H. Sheridan, U. S. A.; Brig. Gen. D. B. Sacket,

U. S. A.; Brig. Gen. M. D. Hardin, U. S. A.; Lieut. Col. M. V. Sheridan, U. S. A.; Lieut. Col. J. F. Gregory, U. S. A.; Gen. W. E. Strong, Chicago; Mr. E. B. Sheldon, Chicago; Mr. Samuel Johnson, Chicago; Dr. William Wesselhoeft, Boston; Mr. William Wesselhoeft, Boston; four servants; Capt. S. C. Kellogg, Fifth Cavalry; First Lieut. G. O. Eaton, Fifth Cavalry; Second Lieut. L. S. Welborn, Fifth Cavalry; Surgeon W. H. Forwood, U. S. A.; one hospital steward; 60 enlisted men, Company I, Fifth Cavalry; 80 horses; Thomas Moore, chief packer; 34 citizen packers; 173 pack mules; 3 horses; J. A. Campbell, scout; 1 interpreter; 2 packers; 10 mules; 5 Crow Indians, and 1 squaw.

RECAPITULATION.

Officers	9
Civilians	5
Enlisted men	61
Packers	37
Scout	1
Interpreter	1
Indians	6
Servants	4
Total	124
Horses	83
Mules	183

The total number of pack animals (mules) was 142. These were divided into trains, as follows:

Headquarters' train	38
Supply and ammunition train	33
Company and officers' train	40
Packers' supplies, rations, &c	21
Scout's party	10

Of these, 48 were provided with Moore's pack-saddles, the rest having aparejos.

August 4, *Thursday.*—At 6.30 a. m. we were on the trail leading up into the Big Horn Mountains. The ascent was very steep, rising 3,000 feet in about 4 miles. The route proposed was to reach the main divide of the mountains and to follow it as near as might be to the boundary line between Wyoming and Montana, anp thence to descend to the Big Horn River at old Fort C. F. Smith. The trail lay to the north of and along the North Fork of Tongue River, on a tributary of which we went into camp at 11.30 a. m.

The difference of temperature between the air of the mountains and that of the valley below was about 25°. On Monday last, at Tongue River, the thermometer stood at 101° at 3 p. m.; to-day at the same hour it was but 76°. Two deer were killed to-day by the Indians. Mr. Wesselhoeft went hunting in the afternoon with the interpreter, and, when about 10 miles from camp, left his horse loose whilst he fired at an antelope. The horse galloped away and came into camp, and his would-be rider was obliged to foot it. There was some uneasiness in camp lest he should be lost, but the fears were dispelled by his arrival about nine o'clock.

Altitude of camp, 7,700 feet; distance marched, 14 miles.

August 5, *Friday.*—There was quite a heavy frost last night, and the grass was heavy and wet with it when we broke camp at 6 a. m. Crossed a low divide to the south shortly after leaving camp, and descending to the valley of the North Fork of Tongue Rirver followed that stream nearly to its source, our general course being from southwest to south. On leaving the North Fork of Tongue River we turned nearly due south to cross the main divide of the mountains, which at the summit has an altitude of 9,100 feet. The summit and the hillsides around are covered with dense mats of wild flowers, and in various directions above and below are to be seen huge banks of last winter's snow. Dr. Forwood, who is our botanist, says that the forget-me-nots, which in the east bloom in May, are just now in bloom here. We camped at the head of a beautiful creek, which cañons about 2 miles below and empties into Shell Creek. Two antelopes and one buffalo were killed in the afternoon. The country evidently has recently been full of game, which has probably been driven further south by the forest fires.

In the afternoon General Sheridan and I rode south and southwest about 3 miles to the western edge of the mountains, which are even more abrupt on the western than the eastern slope. From our point of vantage a magnificent view of the country beyond the Big Horn Range was obtained, and a fair knowledge of its geography acquired. The Wind River and Clark's Fork ranges of mountains were in view, and the course of the Big Horn River, Shell Creek, and its tributaries, the Stinking Water and Grey Bull River, could be traced. The topography of the country, between the crest of the mountains and the Big Horn River, as laid down in the most recent maps is largely imaginary, and no streams flowing into Shell Creek from the northeast are shown at all: whereas we camped on quite a large one, and could see the cañons of others. All around us were tracks and signs of much large game, but we saw no animals. Returning, we found the wreck of a wagon, and were much surprised that a wagon could have been gotten here, but not at all surprised that it was wrecked.

At 6 p. m. the thermometer stood at 54°, and during the evening it was too cold to sit around the camp fire in comfort without overcoats.

Altitude of camp, 8,700 feet; distance marched, 14 miles.

August 6, Saturday.—On the trail at 6.10 a. m., the general direction being northwestwardly and following the main divide. The trail was a very good one, over a lovely mountain country partly timbered, with abundant grass and water. Arrived in camp on a lovely little stream, tributary to the Big Horn, at 10.10 a. m. In the afternoon several of the gentlemen, with some of the scouts, went hunting, the result being ten elk killed, one "silver tip" bear, and a black tail deer. On the march one antelope was killed, and several grouse. Temperature at 2 p. m., 82°: at 10 p. m., 46°. Altitude, 8,500 feet; distance marched, 12 miles.

August 7, Sunday.—Broke camp at 6.15 a. m. On taking the trail out of camp we ascended a very steep hill, and thenceforward all day the trail led us up and down steep places on the divide between Big Horn and Little Big Horn Rivers. The rocks are all limestone, and at numerous places we crossed incipient cañons and caves. The greatest altitude reached during the day was 9,500 feet, a little off the trail and about four miles from camp, where a grand view of the country was had. Soon after leaving this point we came suddenly upon a small herd of horses, and then upon the camp of their owners, who were Englishmen out hunting. They had been here in camp ten days, and, besides several elk and deer, had killed twelve bears. We went into camp shortly after noon at some springs near the head of the cañon of Rotten or Greasy Grass Creek. The springs were dug out to furnish water for camp purposes and the animals sent for water down into the cañon or the creek. It is apparent here that we have left the beautiful mountain country, with its snow-banks and wild flowers, timber and springs, luxuriant grass, and cool streams of crystal clearness, for before us the country looks hard and parched. The grass begins to have more the appearance of the late summer grass of the prairies. There is no timber visible, and water is apparently scarce. It is with much regret we leave these pleasant scenes, for a whole summer could be here spent without tire. Temperature at 5 a. m., 50°; at 2 p. m., 80°. Altitude of camp, 7,500 feet. Distance marched, 19 miles.

August 8, Monday.—On the trail to the north and northwest at 6.20 a. m. At 9 a. m. we reached the edge of the Black Cañon and dismounted to look down into it. The sides are very precipitous and densely covered, except at points, with spruce and pine trees. The cañon at the point where we stood is, probably, 2,000 or more feet deep, and derives its name from the dark color of the timber and the denseness of the shadows. At the bottom of the cañon flows a small stream, Cañon Creek, which empties into the Big Horn. about eight miles above old Fort C. F. Smith. It is said to be a good trout stream.

After leaving the Black Cañon our general direction was north, but we made two long detours, first to the east and then to the west. around some long ridges which lay between us and the Big Horn. We found the country very dry but with abundant grass. A summer shower came upon us during the march, after which the sun came out, and it was extremely hot. We arrived at 1.10 p. m. at the bank of the Big Horn, just above old Fort C. F. Smith, where we went into camp, all pretty well tired because of the long march all the way down hill and the heat and dust. Of old Fort Smith only portions of the old adobe walls remain to mark the site. On a prominent hill near by there is a small cemetery inclosed by a low stone wall, and in it stands a very conspicuous white limestone monument, which marks the last resting-place of one officer, several soldiers and citizens, who were killed here by the Sioux. It is proposed to remove the remains to the national cemetery on the Custer battle-field.

The Big Horn at our camp is about 100 yards wide. It has a very swift current, and is not fordable. We found awaiting our arrival Lieut. A. M. Fuller, Second Cavalry, with Company F of that regiment, on the west bank of the river. They had brought a yawl-boat with them from Fort Custer and had rigged a flying ferry with which to cross persons, equipages, and supplies. The forage and rations and pack-saddles were crossed by the ferry during the afternoon. Whilst on the march two black-tail deer and two antelopes were killed. Temperature at 3 p. m., 89°. Altitude of halting place at the Black Cañon, 6,500 feet. Altitude of camp, which was eight miles down the Big Horn from the mouth of the Black Cañon, 3,300 feet. Distance marched, 23 miles.

August 9, Tuesday.—The day was occupied in swimming the mules and horses across the river and in getting our camps over to the bluffs on the left bank, which was all accomplished without loss by a little afternoon. "Bad Belly," a young Crow Indian, one of our scouts, clad only in a breech-clout, was the genius of the mule and horse swimming business. His method was to lead each bell-animal into the water until he got beyond his depth, when he suddenly changed his front for a rear position, and, grasping the animal by the mane, swam with him, at the same time uttering peculiar and piercing cries to urge him to swim for the opposite shore. The herds were driven in by the herders, and generally followed their leader. Sometimes, in spite of all efforts, the herd, upon losing their footing, persisted in and succeeded in returning to the starting point, when the whole operation had to be repeated. "Bad Belly" was almost constantly in the water for about three hours, and swam the river many times, returning by the ferry. He appeared

to be none the worse for it after it was over, and seemed proud of the
fact that his amphibiousness was much admired by all of the white
people.

The day was the hottest we have had since leaving Tongue River.
Temperature 96° at 3 p. m. General A. J. Alexander and Capt. G.
K. Sanderson came from Fort Custer in the afternoon to remain over
night. Mr. Johnson of our party, who has been quite ill for a few days,
has determined, by the advice of our doctors, to give up the trip and
go to Fort Custer to-morrow with General Alexander and Captain Sanderson, returning thence to Chicago. The doctors think he might go
on, but that if he were worse there would be no means of caring for
him.

Our camp is on the gravel and dirt; there is very little grass and the
tent-pins cannot be driven very far.

August 10, *Wednesday.*—Broke camp on the west bank of the Big
Horn rather sooner than was pleasant this morning. It was hot in the
early part of the night, and, about two in the morning began to blow
furiously from the south, bringing clouds of dust and fine gravel, to our
great discomfort. Some of the tents blew down, and by four o'clock we had
taken the rest down to save them. Breakfast was very scarce and very
dirty, and we were all glad to get started westward, as we did, at 6.25
a. m. Mr. Johnson remained behind to return to Chicago, via Fort
Custer, Glendive, and the Northern Pacific Railroad. The general direction of our trail was a little south of west, along the north slope of
Pryor's Mountains. We arrived in camp, on a fork of Beauvais Creek,
at 11.45 a. m. We have a very clean, pretty camping place, with an
abundance of grass, and enough wood for our use—quite in contrast to
yesterday's dirty camp. The wind still blows fresh from the south, but
there is no dust. Altitude of camp, 4,400 feet; distance, 18 miles.

August 11, *Thursday.*—On the trail westward at 6.10 a. m. We followed the trail for a distance and then left it, turning to the south to
go further up in the mountain side. We had better have kept the trail,
for we found it a hard pull up the mountain and a bad pitch down
again. Fortunately it has been a pleasant day for marching. There is
a Crow camp of about sixty lodges about ten miles down the West
Fork of Pryor's Creek, and their lodges were plainly visible from the
trail to-day, about eight miles to our right hand. Arrived in camp on
West Fork of Pryor's Creek at 11.50 a. m., where in the afternoon great
numbers of handsome trout were taken. This is said to be one of the
best trout streams in the whole country. Maximum temperature to-
day, 82°; altitude, 4,400 feet; distance, 19 miles.

August 12, *Friday.*—Broke camp at 6.06 a. m. and traveled south-
wardly through Pryor's Gap. At the entrance to Pryor's Gap there are
numerous large heaps of rocks which mark the site of a battle between
the Sioux and Crows about seven years ago, in which Bad Belly partici-
pated. After passing through the gap. our general course was west
until we struck a road at the head of the ravine of Red Willow Creek.
Thence we followed the road and the windings of the steep and tortuous
ravine until we reached its mouth, when we left the road and marched
southwest until we reached Clark's Fork, where, at 1.05 p. m., we went
into camp on an island. The road we followed is said to be the only
passable trail through this country of Bad Lands. The grass on the
island was long and rank and our camp was almost buried it it. It was
not a pleasant place, but every one was tired with the long, hot, and
dusty march, and not disposed to seek a better camp, if indeed it were
possible to find one. No game was seen during the day, if I except a

jack-rabbit which our dog Bruin chased out of sight. Temperature at 3 p. m., 86°. Altitude, 3,700 feet; distance, 25 miles.

August 13, *Saturday.*—Broke camp at 5.30 a. m. From here-it had been intended to take the road made by General Sturgis, when in pursuit of the Nez Perces Indians, to the debouche of Clark's Fork from the mountains; but the road crosses Clark's Fork four times, and now the river is not fordable, being very high and with a current of about ten miles per hour. So we were obliged to make a trail around and through the Bad Lands, which we found difficult, hot, and dusty.

We went into camp behind a Bad Lands' bluff, on Clark's Fork, at 11.40 a. m. One elk was killed by a soldier on the west side of Clark's Fork in the afternoon. Several tried the fishing but caught nothing. Temperature at 2 p. m., 96°. Altitude at camp, 4,250 feet; distance, 19 miles.

August 14, *Sunday* —This morning we set our watches back twenty-five minutes to correspond more nearly to the true time in this longitude. On the trail at 6.20 a. m., going very nearly due south. The maps appear to be all wrong in the vicinity of the mouth of Clark's Fork Cañon. Bennett's Creek comes down close to the edge of the mountains until within a couple of miles of the mouth of Clark's Fork Cañon, when it turns abruptly to the east and empties into Clark's Fork eight or ten miles below the cañon. We crossed Pat O'Hara's Creek at 10.30 a. m. This is not given on the map. It runs, in a deep ravine, nearly north, and empties into Clark's Fork, as does the creek next west of it, which we crossed at 11.10 a. m. This latter creek is also in a deep ravine and flows parallel to Pat O'Hara's Creek.

Clark's Fork on emerging from the cañon makes a bend to the south and then a big bend to the east, north, and west, making nearly three-quarters of a circle before it assumes its general northerly direction. A ridge of high red rocks blocks the mouth of the cañon, most of the ridge lying to the north of the cañon, and around the south end of this the river bends. We camped on Red Creek, the smallest of the streams flowing into Clark's Fork; it comes down from the mountains, behind a ridge or comb of white rock, which is parallel to the general direction of the mountains, and flows almost straight north. To-day and yesterday were about the most disagreeable marches of the trip thus far, on account of the heat and dust. One antelope killed this afternoon by Bad Belly. Altitude of camp, 5,150 feet; distance marched, 22 miles.

August 15, *Monday.*—From here on, Moore is to be our guide, as he was over the trail last season with the honorable Secretary of the Interior. Moore says that just under the red ridge, near our camp, Mr. Schurz and two others killed three bears at one shot from each of their rifles, fired simultaneously. Our trail leads to the south and southwest, zigzagging up the steep face of the mountain that has been a landmark to us since yesterday morning. Upon arriving at the top of the first mountain, our eyes were treated to a view not surpassed, if equaled, for variety of scenery by any of the trip. To the east the whole range of the Big Horn Mountains were beautiful in their blue and hazy indistinctness. Between us and them the valleys of the Big Horn and its tributaries, a rough, rugged country, seemed like a vast plain, with pretty little streams winding through it.

Nearer to us, towards the south and southeast, are Cedar and Hart Mountains—landmarks for many miles around; around to the west, a rugged, broken mass, through which it seemed impracticable to penetrate; and to the north, near enough to have all the details and coloring brought out with line-engraving distinctness, the jagged, rocky piles about Clark's Fork Cañon. A little farther to the westward we came to the "jumping off place," where we made a descent of 1,900 feet, to the bed of Dead Indian Creek, in about three-quarters of a mile in distance. There we obtained a view of the wonderful fortification-like formation, which looks indeed like a gigantic fortress with outlying batteries. In our party it was christened "Jerusalem," because of a resemblance, noted by many of us, to the famous painting of the ancient fortifications which inclosed the holy city.

We arrived in camp on the unnamed creek next west of Dead Indian Creek a little after noon, enthusiastic about and inspirited by the grand scenery surrounding us, but with knees a little shaky by reason of walking and sliding down the steep declivity spoken of, and at the same time managing our horses so they might not fall atop of us should their footing give way. We had three showers during the day, two whilst on the trail, and one after we had gotten into camp. Temperature at 2 p. m., 86°; distance marched, 11 miles.

August 16, *Tuesday.*—On the trail at 6.15 a. m. Crossed the creek, on which we encamped, below its forks with another unnamed creek, and soon after crossed the South Fork of Clark's Fork, at a bad ford which is full of big bowlders. Some of the mules got down in the rush of waters, but no serious damage was done. The mule with our medicine chest "aboard" got down, but fortunately was gotten out before it had time to soak.

South Fork was very muddy, as if there had been recent and heavy rains in the mountains. We passed close by "Jerusalem," and instead of the likeness to fortifications being dispelled by a nearer view it seemed almost as great as from a distance. Thence the trail winds around the mountain and through heavy timber to avoid marshy places. This trail is the one pursued by Chief Joseph and the Nez Percés in their famous flight in 1878. Some considerable trees had fallen across it, which our packers cleared out to let our trains pass. After getting out of the timber our general bearing was west. We passed through a large basin in which there were several lakes with numerous wild fowl on them, and around which there were plenty of fresh game trails. Went into camp at 11.10 a. m. on a small unnamed creek, which flows north into Crandall Creek, about a quarter of mile from its mouth. It rained here during the forenoon and again in the afternoon, but cleared in the afternoon. After it cleared the mountains around us were seen to be covered with freshly-fallen snow. The Beartooth Range to the north of us are covered with enormous glaciers. Colonel Sheridan, General Story, and Mr. Sheldon, with some guides and several packs, started about 3 p. m. for a grand hunt in the vicinity of Deep Lake, about 12 miles to the north. They purpose remaining out over night to get the early morning opportunities. Altitude of camp 6,500 feet. Distance marched, 15 miles.

August 17, *Wednesday.*—Remained in camp overhauling and repacking supplies, making tent pins, &c. Several of the party went out hunting during the day, the capture being one antelope. Towards night Colonel Sheridan and party came in bringing with them the carcasses of six elks. They report having seen late in the evening a band of at least 150 elks disporting themselves and bathing in a lake about a mile long. Of these they killed seven, but one came to his death so far out in the cold lake that they were unable to get him. Unfortunately their horns are "in the velvet," and not fit for preservation. We have now enough elk meat to last a long time, and there is no danger of its soon

2 SH

spoiling in this altitude. Water in the buckets froze a quarter of an inch thick during the night.

August 18, *Thursday.*—On the trail at 6.15 a. m. The general direction to-day was northwest and on the mountain sides up the valley of the North Fork of Clark's Fork, which we twice came down to. The rest of the march was high up on the mountain sides, following the bed of a small creek, which we crossed several times. Went into camp on North Fork almost under the shadow of Pilot Peak.

The game killed during the day consists of one jack-rabbit slain by a soldier. It rained hard in the afternoon and snowed on the mountains. After the storm it was cold, wet, and disagreeable. A roaring camp fire in the evening contributed much to our comfort. Altitude 6,700 feet. Distance travelled, 13 miles.

August 19, *Friday.*—On the trail at 6.10 a. m. The ascent to the divide between Clark's Fork and Soda Butte Creek is very steep; the altitude of the summit being 7,800 feet. In about eleven miles traveling we arrived at Cook City, a mining camp on the Crow Indian Reservation, which has attracted much attention in the northwest, and has been the subject of considerable discussion in the public press. Cook City possesses one habitable house and perhaps twenty in all stages of construction, as well as a smelter; plenty of town lots. We had some conversation with a Mr. Dewey, who has lived there for the past nine years, and from his statements I cull the following: The district of mines, about one hundred in all, is embraced within a radius from Cook City of a very few miles. Of them the Clark's Fork and Great Republic mines are, so far as known, the richest; and some ores from them have yielded from one thousand to fifteen hundred dollars per ton. When the mines were prospected and working them began, they were supposed to be located on the public lands of Wyoming; but the survey of the boundary line between Wyoming and Montana, made last year, developed the fact that they were in Montana, and consequently on the Crow Indian Reservation. This of course stopped the working of the mines and the smelter. The claimants to the mines, some of them, still remain by their claims, and others who are not there are laboring to effect some relief by means of an act of Congress. It would seem to be just and beneficial to the government, as well as to individuals, that Congress should purchase these mineral lands from the Crows and throw them open to the people, especially as they are of no use to the Indians, who, since they have been part of their reservation, have never been known to visit them.

We camped on Soda Butte Creek, nine miles below the smelter. The day has been bright and cold, and the march an extremely pleasant one. Altitude of camp, 7,100 feet. Distance marched, 20 miles.

August 20, *Saturday.*—Broke camp at 6.10 a. m., and traveled on the road down Soda Butte Creek for eight miles, when we went into camp. Soda Butte, which is near and gives its name to the creek, is a limestone crater deposit from the bubbling soda springs, about twenty feet high. It is about one mile below where we camped. Above, about half a mile, and behind a ridge so that it is not visible from the road, is Soda Butte Lake, in which, we had been informed, there were multitudes of fine trout. It is said that the miners of Cook City took ten tons out of it last fall by drawing the lake and using nets, and dried them for winter's use. We tried both the lake and the creek, and had but indifferent success, though enough were taken to supply our table.

My pocket thermometer was broken about a week ago, and therefore temperatures have not since been recorded, except occasionally, by means of a troublesome maximum thermometer. Altitude, 6,450 feet. Distance, 8 miles.

August 21, Sunday.—Broke camp at 6.10 a. m., and traveled down the road along Soda Butte Creek, stopping for a few moments at Soda Butte. Soon after we left the road, which crosses the creek to the south, and keeping on the north side, followed a trail around the brow of a mountain, effecting a slight saving of distance. About eight miles from camp we crossed the creek and took the old road. Crossed the Yellowstone River by Baronett's bridge, and went into camp at the head of a small creek three-quarters of a mile west of the river, and about a mile above the bridge. Mr. Sacket, a brother of General Sacket, from Helena, with a friend of his, joined us on the road about four miles east of Baronett's bridge. Altitude of camp, 6,250 feet. Distance, 17 miles.

August 22, Monday.—Jack Baronett, the proprietor of the bridge, and the most famous guide and hunter of this country, joined us this morning, and is to accompany us on our journey as far as the Geyser Basins. There are two trails from the bridge to the Yellowstone Falls, the newer one being nearest to the river. Baronett said that it had been newly opened and he had not been over it, and that the old trail was likely to be, at present, the best, so the old one was followed. Leaving camp at 6.20 a. m., we arrived at Tower Falls in about an hour, where we stopped to view the Falls, but did not go below them. At 9 a. m. we left the trail to the Falls for the ascent of Mount Washburne, which we accomplished nearly all the way on horseback (and it could easily be so done all the way) in three-quarters of an hour. The height of Mount Washburne is variously given by different authorities. My barometer read 9,950 feet. It is not far from 10,000 feet above the sea. The wind blew furiously and cold whilst we were on the summit, so we remained but half an hour. The view from the summit is a very comprehensive one, and embraces the entire perimeter of one of the largest lakes in the world that has so great an altitude, Yellowstone Lake.

In a cairn of stones on the summit we found a tin box containing the names of many distinguished people who have been there. We carefully replaced the box, inclosing in it also the names of the members of our party, including those of our Crow scouts, Bad Belly, and Bob-tail-crow, much to their delight.

We did not make the descent by the trail, but went down, without accident, on the south side of the mountain, a very steep declivity and covered with loose rocks. At noon we arrived at the Devil's Caldron, and at 2 p. m. at Point Lookout, whence a fine view of the grand cañon of the Yellowstone is had. We arrived at the Lower Falls at 2.30 p. m., where we found General Sacket had pitched our camp. He had made the ascent of Mt. Washburne in 1875 and did not care to do it again, so went around with the train. As we were returning from the top of the Lower Falls we met a party of tourists from Helena, whose pack-horse loaded with their provisions had run away through the timber and scattered their rations beyond hope of recovery. They were, therefore, on very short allowance, and were pleased to receive some elk meat and other things to last them until they could reach the Lower Geyser Basin, where more could be obtained. Altitude of camp 7,625 feet. Distance traveled, 25 miles. Distance traveled by the pack train, 20 miles.

August 23, Tuesday.—On the trail to Mud Geyser at 6.10 a. m. We stopped by the way to see Sulphur Mountain, where there is one large, active, boiling mud geyser and a whole mountain side of small spouts, and went into camp on the Yellowstone, near Mud Geyser, at 9.45 a. m.

The geyser disappointed us, as its spout was only four or five feet high, whereas we had expected to see a column of mud thrown at least thirty feet. During the rest of the day some of the party visited Yellowstone Lake, about seven miles distant, and the rest went fishing in the Yellowstone.

The trout in the river above the falls are all wormy, whilst those below the falls are not so affected: a fact which no scientist has, so far as I know, attempted to explain. There are boiling springs close to the bank of the river, where one can stand and catch a fish and cook him by the simple process of lifting him from the river and depositing him in the spring. We did not try that; but some of us bathed in the river, where the overflow from some hot springs empties into it, which so modifies the cold water of the river that one can have a very comfortable bath. Altitude of camp, 7,525 feet. Distance traveled, 8 miles.

August 24, Wednesday.—There was a heavy frost last night, and this morning the day is bright, and the air cold and bracing. On the way at 6.10 a. m., as usual, and took the trail westward for the Lower Geyser Basin. A few miles out we met two wagons and a party of road-makers, who are nearly at the end of their work of completing a good road from the Geyser Basin to the Mud Geyser. They are also to make the trail thence to Yellowstone Lake a wagon-road, so that in a couple of weeks tourists to the Geyser Basin will be able to continue their journeys by wagon through to the lake. At 8.45 a. m. we crossed Alum Creek (so strongly impregnated that animals will not touch it), and an hour later reached Sulphur Lake, where we remained a quarter of an hour examining the mud and sulphur geysers. Reached Lake Mary at 10 a. m., where we watered the stock. The lake is circular, about a quarter of a mile in diameter, and is closely engirdled with dense spruce and pine timber. Its altitude is 8,100 feet.

Crossed the East Fork of Firehole River several times, and went into camp at 1.15 p. m. near Fountain Geyser, the largest of the Lower Basin group. The rest of the day was spent in examining the boiling springs and geysers, and the curious boiling clay-geyser called the Paint Pots. The fountain played at 5.48 p. m., its exhibition lasting forty-two minutes. Distance traveled, 24 miles.

August 25, Thursday.—Broke camp at 6.15 a. m., and took the road for the Upper Geyser Basin. At 7.15 a. m. we crossed to the west side of the Firehole River to see the large geyser which until this year had only been considered a boiling spring, but which this year has made several eruptions, throwing out with the water a large amount of stony materials. Arrived at the Upper Basin at 9.15 a. m., and went into camp in a lovely pine grove about 150 yards from "Old Faithful." We met to-day several parties of tourists from Virginia City and Helena camped at various places in the basin. Grass is rather scarce for an outfit so large as ours, but it will have to do for this afternoon's and to-morrow's grazing. Campbell came in towards evening with our mail from Fort Ellis, whither he had been sent from Baronett's Bridge. He has ridden from Mammoth Hot Springs to-day, 70 miles.

August 26, Friday.—Remained in camp. Yesterday afternoon was principally occupied in watching Old Faithful, whose regularity of eruption makes her, perhaps, the most interesting of the group. On yesterday and to-day we have seen play all of the large geysers of the group except the Giant and Giantess. To-day we visited them on horse-back, and were rewarded by seeing many of them play. Yesterday the Grand played twice, but we were half a mile away; so to-day we went over to it at 3 p. m., and sat around on the rocks and under the trees until 5.45 p. m., when our patience was rewarded by a grand display. There were eight distinct eruptions, the latter ones higher but of briefer duration than the earlier ones, and the total time of eruption was 22 minutes. The aperture is about 4 feet in diameter, and the height to which the water is thrown is said to be over 200 feet. Yesterday and to-day we have seen eruptions of the following named geysers, some of them more than once, and Old Faithful a great many times. viz: Fountain, Old Faithful, Bee-Hive, Lion, Lioness, Castle, and Splendid.

Our men made Old Faithful useful as well as ornamental by throwing their soiled clothes into the crater during the period of quiescence. With the eruption, which occurs every sixty-five or sixty-seven minutes, the clothes are thrown high in the air—two hundred or more feet, and when picked up are found to be perfectly washed. Cotton and linen clothes were not injured, but woolen shirts and pants were usually torn to shreds.

As we rode from geyser to geyser over crusts of rock which betoken, by the hollow sound of the horses' footsteps and by the spurts of hot water and jets of steam constantly and everywhere exhibited, the thinness of the stratum between us and the caverns below, the curious fact that the horses did not mind these things at all could not fail to be impressed upon one. They stood with wide open eyes and pricked forward ears within, sometimes, a hundred feet or so of an eruptive geyser—an awe-inspiring spectacle to man—without betraying any appearance of fear.

Mr. Norris, the superintendent of the park, is doing a good work in making wagon-roads to the principal points of interest and trails to the less important ones. If in addition some means could be devised to stop and prevent the vandalism which seems to pervade the average American citizen, and restrain his or her, especially *her*, propensities to hammer and chip off rocks, to break down and destroy every growing thing, and to fill up with trees, sticks, &c., the wonderful craters, a great indebtedness would be felt by every person appreciative of these greatest natural wonders of the world. The beauty of Old Faithful's crater as well as that of the other geysers has been greatly marred in this way, and the work of destruction is rapidly going on. We saw persons with hatchets who were hammering and cracking the beautiful tracery around the geysers, without even the poor excuse of obtaining specimens, as they did not take away what they broke off. They destroyed for the pleasure they had in their work.

August 27, Saturday.—Went to take a last look at Old Faithful at 5.30 a. m. On the road at 6.05 a. m. Arrived at Forks of the Firehole River at 9.05 a. m. Crossed the West Fork, and went into camp about a half-mile above the hotel of the Lower Geyser Basin. There was a large fire in the timber south and west of the hotel, and the latter came very near to being burned yesterday. We were obliged to watch the fire behind our camp, and to fight it back when it approached too near. Altitude, 7,200 feet. Distance traveled, 11 miles.

August 28, Sunday.—Broke camp at 6.15 a. m., and traveled west by the road over the divide through Sure-enough Forest, and down Norris' Slide. Arrived at the stage station on Madison River at 9.40 a. m. The road from the Geyser Basin to Henry's Lake is part of the stage road to Virginia City; but no stages have as yet been regularly put on the route; and we found no one at the station, though there was an old stage there.

The road for a long distance winds around through the openings of the pine trees, being much longer than is necessary, to save labor and clearing.

Arrived in camp on the left bank of the West Fork of Madison River at 12.40 p. m.

During the afternoon several fish of about a pound weight were caught, which, by the experts of the party, were said to be grayling. Altitude, 6,650 feet. Distance traveled, 24 miles.

August 29, Monday.—Broke camp at 6.10 a. m., and followed the road over Tahgee Pass. The pass has an altitude of only 7,050 feet, and it is so low and wide that one might pass over the summit without realizing it unless on the alert. After descending from the pass, we left the Virginia City road and followed the track of a few wagons to the south, across a low grassy plain, which, in early summer, must be very soft and swampy. Crossed Henry's Fork of the Snake River at 9.45 a. m., and went into camp at the second crossing of the same stream at 11.40 a. m. We passed within about 3 miles of Henry's Lake, which is a lovely sheet of water hemmed in on three sides by the Divide of the Continent. It is said to abound in fish, and its surface to be covered at seasons with all kinds of water fowl. During the afternoon the fishermen of the party had fine sport with the trout in Henry's Fork. The fish are abundant and fine, but the stream is broad, and shallow near the banks, affording few pools, so that a boat or raft is necessary to great success. All agreed, however, that there was more trout in it than in any stream we had seen; 153 were caught.

August 30, Tuesday.—Broke camp at 6.15 a. m., and went west about a mile when we again forded Henry's Fork, and traveled nearly south, east of the cañon, to the third crossing of Henry's Fork. Thence we crossed a small divide between Potter and Shotgun Creeks, and followed up the course of the Slough Fork of Shotgun Creek. Slough Fork, as its name implies, spreads over a wide country, which is low and marshy, and its pools were full of ducks and geese. At Slough Fork we came upon Howard's road, made by General Howard when in pursuit of the Nez Percés, and followed it for a distance over a sage-brush prairie. Then, as it appeared tortuous, we left it and traveled though the sage brush, with no trail, to our camp on Slough Fork, where we arrived at 12.45 p. m. During the afternoon we had fine sport catching trout, which, though small, were game. Altitude, 6,400 feet. Distance traveled, 22 miles.

August 31, Wednesday.—Broke camp at 6.25 a. m., and traveled in a general westerly direction, winding around amongst low hills for about 9 miles. Then we descended to the prairie, passing about a half-mile to the north of Camas Springs. The rest of the distance to our camp, at the forks of Camas Creek, was over, first, a sage brush, and then a grass prairie. At the West Fork of Camas Creek there is a large hay ranch, where a man was seen driving a mowing-machine. Thinking he might have some late news about the condition of President Garfield, of whom we had not heard in several days, one of the party rode over and asked him the question: "Have you any late news about the President?" To which the reply was: "*What* President?" Disgusted and not desiring to continue the conversation on that subject, he essayed another: "Have you shot any grouse around here?" This time the answer was more satisfactory: "Yes, we've killed *quite a few.*"

The afternoon was passed fishing and shooting sage chickens. Some ducks were also obtained, and one antelope. Altitude of camp, 6,200 feet. Distance marched, 18 miles.

September 1, Thursday.—There was no wood for a camp fire last night or this morning. Only enough dry willow bushes were gotten for cooking purposes, and as the morning was cold and the grass wet with frost, we were glad to mount and get started on our way. Left camp at 6.15 a. m., and traveled nearly due south for about four miles, where we struck the wagon road for Camas Station, and followed it the rest of the march. Our way was down Camas Creek, and for the last half of the march was over lava fields. Arrived in camp on Camas Creek at 10.25 a. m., where there was said to be good fishing; few, however, were caught. There was plenty of dry red cedar to make a good camp fire, so we passed a very pleasant evening.

From the rise of ground just back of camp the windmill at Camas Station, on the Utah and Northern Railroad, can be seen. It is to be the terminus of our journey on horseback. Distance traveled, 14 miles.

September 2, Friday.—We were on the road at 6.30 a. m. It was very good for about 6 miles, and the rest of the way into Camas it was very sandy and disagreeable. The road follows the creek and bends about 3 miles to the right of the straight line from our camp to Camas.

Arrived and made camp on the creek near the railway station at 10.10 a. m. Altitude of Camas Station, 4,925 feet. Distance traveled, 14 miles.

At Camas we left Colonel Kellogg with his command, including the pack trains and equipage, to march to Fort Laramie via the Teton Pass and Wind River to Fort Washakie, and thence by the road to Laramie. Our party took the evening south-bound train of the Utah and Northern Railroad, and the next morning the east-bound train of the Union Pacific Railroad from Ogden, arriving in Chicago on the afternoon of September 6.

General Sheridan left us at Cheyenne to return to Chicago by way of Denver and Pueblo, Colo.

During the trip we made 29 camps. reckoning from Tongue River, and traveled 288 miles by wagons, and 336 miles on horseback.

REPORT OF CAPT. S. C. KELLOGG.

FORT LARAMIE, WYO., *September 28, 1881.*

GENERAL: I have the honor to report the following march of Company I, Fifth Cavalry, with pack-mule transportation, from Camas Station, on the Utah Northern Railway, in Idaho, to Fort Washakie, in Wyoming Territory.

September 3.—Left Camas by a trail of our own making. which intersected a wagon-road about 9 miles from the town, which wagon-road runs eastward over sandy hills to the Mormon settlement of Egin on Henry's Fork of Snake River.

Went up river 2 miles to a good camp in river bottom, about one-half mile below Eagle Nest Ford.

Egin is a settlement of 10 Mormon families, who have come there from Utah within the past 3 years. It is a duly authorized post-office, the mail being brought weekly by private carrier from Camas, no post-route having yet been established. Distance from Camas to Egin, 23 miles by road. An easier route, and more free from heavy sand, is to Market Lake. by a road following down Snake River, and the distance between the two places is about the same as it is to Camas.

Roads lead from Egin on both sides of Snake River northward to ranches on Snake River and its affluents.

These Mormons intend taking out a ditch that will irrigate the whole valley near their settlement; they already cut a plentiful supply of hay on the bottoms nearest the river.

A practicable but somewhat deep ford exists right at Egin, although it is not used as much as the Eagle Nest Ford, 2½ miles above, on account of the latter being always shallow.

Below this Egin Ford none of the crossings of Snake River are safe. Egin is the Shoshone word for "cold."

The distance from Egin to Eagle-Rock Bridge, the railroad crossing of Snake River, is 40 miles via Adams' Ranch, on Market Lake, by a road which follows Snake River the entire distance.

September 4.—Crossed river at Eagle Nest Ford, the water in deepest place not wetting horses' bellies, and made our own trail nearly due east over sandy slopes to a point on Pierre's River, 6 miles. The local names for this stream, as well as for Pierre's Hole, at the foot of the Tetons, are Teton Fork and Teton Basin. The other names are unknown to the people of the vicinity.

Followed up north side of Teton Fork, a good-sized stream, to a point about 30 miles from its mouth, where a crossing was effected on the 5th above the main cañon. Here a good trail was found coming from the north from towards Fall or Conant River, and is supposed to be originally one of Captain Reynold's trails, as it leads into the Teton Basin. One is, however, liable to confound it with the many game trails that cover the whole region.

At a point about 14 miles above its mouth, the Teton Fork Cañon deepens for a distance of about 15 miles, the only point at which it can be crossed there being where I crossed it on the old Raynold's trail, unless a crossing be made below the cañon at or near the cabin of a trapper named Tom Lavering, who, with Beaver Dick, is spoken of as the best guide obtainable for the Teton country. The cañon of the Teton Fork is exceedingly beautiful and deep, with precipitate sides generally, although in many places sufficient slope is afforded for pine timber to grow. If the Teton is crossed at or near Lavering's, a nearer route is afforded into the Teton Basin by a trail on its west side than the one taken by me down and through the center of the basin from the north end of it.

The Teton Basin is 25 miles long by about 10 wide, closely shut in by high mountain ranges on all sides except the north; there are two outlets to the south, one towards the southwest, as reported by the Shoshone Indians, who occasionally come there to hunt from Fort Hall, and the other is the Teton Pass, at the southeastern corner, where is also the head of the Teton Fork or Pierre's River proper.

That part of the Teton River crossed by me at the north end of the basin is known as the North Fork.

The basin is traversed from east to west by five well-timbered streams of running water (feeders of Teton River) at intervals of about 5 miles, and these intervals are fine grassy plains that in summer, at least, might furnish excellent pasturage for cattle; but solitude reigns supreme, with scarcely any wild animals even to disturb it.

It is said that trappers come into the basin occasionally, but we saw no signs of any having been there lately, and, as we could get but very meager information concerning the Teton country from those living nearest to it on Snake River, it may almost be considered a *terra incognita*.

Trappers who are reported to have wintered in the basin found the snow deep on the level, and, in consequence, it may not be deemed a suitable range for grazing purposes. Although said to be a fine elk country, we saw only a few antelope.

Both during the 5th and 6th September, whilst we were in the basin, we could not see the Grand Teton Peaks that we knew were towering into the clouds immediately over us, for although sunny and clear in the valley, the mountains seemed to attract storms that hid them entirely from view; and the spongy nature of the soil towards the Teton River, on the west side, gave evidence of the existence at all times of more or less rain or snowfall in this wonderful *cul-de-sac.*

We left the basin by the Teton Pass on a very good trail, which follows up the Teton River nearly to its head and then leaves it to cross a very steep but short divide at the extreme eastern end of the pass; the pass is so straight in its general course that on looking back as you ascend the divide, you can see 10 miles to your rear into the basin.

On reaching the summit of the divide, and where your descent into Jackson's Hole commences, a magnificent view of the valley of Snake and Gros Ventre Rivers is afforded as a reward for your hard climbing, and then two hours' steady marching brings you onto the banks of the main Snake River, at the foot of the pass, and immediately opposite the southern extremity of Lower Gros Ventre Butte.

Jackson's Hole appears to be as little known as is the Teton Basin, except, perhaps, to a small number of trappers or Indians. Here, too, the mountain scenery is strikingly grand and majestic.

The solitude is perfect and unbroken, except by the cries of water-fowl or the splashing of trout.

The Snake is here a larger stream, with a much wider bed, than is the Platte in Nebraska at its forks; it flows close under the Tetons and then sweeps away into the wilderness to the southwest, around the mountains bearing its name, literally hearing no sound save its own lashings.

Snake River is easily forded at this season of the year, but from the appearance of its bed it is an impassable torrent when full. A crossing which fronted our camp was used, and immediately on reaching the east bank we struck into the well-marked Shoshone trail from Fort Hall to Fort Washakie, which follows the bend of Snake River westward. After crossing the southern spur of Lower Gros Ventre Butte the trail passes into and through a wide grassy valley that opens into the valley of the Gros Ventre River, a considerable stream with a very wide bed and heavily-timbered banks, which the trail crosses and follows along its north shore, towards and under upper Gros Ventre Butte, until the valley closes at the cañon of the Gros Ventre, about 17 miles from its junction with Snake River. At the cañon our camp of September 7 was made, and from there we were amply repaid for our loss of view in the Teton Basin of the Grand Tetons.

As the storm which had been prevailing in the mountains for the past three days dispersed, the clouds rolled up as does a curtain and revealed the Tetons in all their grandeur. With a faultlessly clear blue sky for a background, five immense pinnacles of rock tower up into the air many thousands of feet above the timber line, the crevices between the pinnacles filled with snow recently fallen. The third or center pinnacle is considerably the largest of the five, and all are gracefully outlined. It is doubtful if a handsomer grouping of mountain peaks exists anywhere, and the name given them by the voyageur who discovered them was aptly chosen. With such a view to feast the eye, and such a valley teeming with trout, game, and water-fowl, an artist having a sportsman-like turn would pronounce Jackson's Hole Paradise. And if an artist would be enraptured by the Tetons in daylight, camping under their shadow, as we were, how intense would be his delight if he could have shared our good fortune to see a full moon light them up after the sun had finished exhibiting them.

The valley of the Gros Ventre narrows into a cañon at intervals of ten or fifteen miles, with occasional open spaces where excellent camps can be obtained. The Shoshone trail follows the windings of the stream, sometimes crossing the spur of a mountain, but always on easy grades. At a point 40 miles from Snake River, a large fork or branch comes in from the south, and here, too, the trail forks; the trail to the right, coming eastward, turns south towards the head of Green River and thence eastward again through Union Pass of Wind River Mountains. The other trail turns off from the Gros Ventre 3 miles further up stream, follows Fish Creek 4 miles nearly due north, and then turns abruptly east up into a pass over the Wind River Mountains, said to be much easier than the Union Pass, and by which you come out onto Wind River by following down a fine large stream, running through a large valley called the West or South Fork of Wind River. It was this unnamed pass we used, and we found it quite easy and practicable. The distance from the Gros Ventre across to Wind River we found to be about 35 miles.

As we approached the point where the trail separates on the Gros Ventre, I was surprised to find a fresh wagon track, which I traced to where it turned southward towards Green River. A trapper from Fort Washakie, or Lander, named Hardin, came into my last camp on the Gros Ventre and informed me the wagon track had been made by some miners, who had hauled a load of sluice boxes from the old railroad-tie camp on Green River to some placers on the Gros Ventre they were working.

The old railroad-tie camp is near the head or bend of Green River, and, no doubt, is an easy route from the railroad to the Gros Ventre region.

September 11 found us on the main Wind River, at Torrey's cattle corral, at the mouth of the West Fork, and at the intersection of the Jones trail to Two-go-tee Pass. Wind River, at the point we struck it, is a small, untimbered stream, but several large feeders come into it from both north and south during its course of 56 miles from that point to Bull Lake Fork, where we left it, a large river, to march over to Fort Washakie, 18 miles across country, by a trail that also runs northward through the Owl Creek Mountains to the Stinking Water and Clark's Fork.

The command reached Fort Washakie September 14, the twelfth march from Camas, and, as near as we could estimate it, the distance between these two points is 260 miles.

At Camas I was furnished with two Shoshone Indians for guides, one of whom, To-sa-co-va-nat-se, had been over part of the trail in 1878, when he was captured, with some hostile Bannocks, and taken into Washakie a prisoner. The other guide, Bannock Frank, knew nothing whatever of the country, but, as he spoke English quite well, he proved useful as interpreter for his comrade.

With the exception of great numbers of antelope and a few bear, we saw no large game, although the country, in many places, especially on the Wind River Mountains, was fairly cut up into elk tracks, and undoubtedly there are vast numbers of them to be found at the proper season. Trout abound in all the streams, and ducks, geese, and cranes are constantly to be seen. Antelope are more abundant than in any section I have ever visited, and the trappers say beaver also are plentiful. The country is still a wilderness, but is too beautiful to remain so much longer.

I have the honor to append a table of distances and a tracing of the route followed.

I am, general, very respectfully, your obedient servant,
S. C. KELLOGG,
Captain, Fifth Cavalry.

Lieutenant-General P. H. SHERIDAN, *U. S. A.*

DISTANCES.

	Miles.
Camas to Egin (Snake River)	23
Egin to Eagle Nest Ford	2½
Eagle Nest Ford to foot of Tetons	47½
Length of Teton Basin	26
Length of Teton Pass	12
Outlet of pass to Shoshone trail	6
Gros Ventre River to Fish Creek	41
Fish Creek to Wind River Pass	16
Wind River Pass to Torrey's Corral	15
Torrey's Corral to Fort Washakie	75
	264

Good camping places westward from Fort Washakie :

Bull Lake Fork, on Wind River	18
Dry Creek, on Wind River	12
North Fork of Wind River	20
West or South Fork of Wind River	24
Foot of pass on South Fork of Wind River	11
Fish Creek, near Gros Ventre	25
Crossing of Gros Ventre	19
West end Gros Ventre Pass	10
Mouth of Gross Ventre	15
West end Teton Pass	18
Bear River, Teton Basin	16
Crossing North Fork Teton River	10
Teton River below Cañon	20
Eagle Nest Ford, Snake River	17
Camas	25
	260

REPORT OF SURGEON W. H. FORWOOD.

FORT OMAHA, NEBR., *September* 10, 1881.

SIR: I have the honor to report that, while serving as medical officer with the Lieutenant-General of the Army, on his recent extended reconnaissance through the Territories of Wyoming and Montana, I have, in addition to my other duties, taken an interest in the flora of the country passed over, and made such observations and collections of specimens as was practicable during rapid and continuous marches without wagon transportation.

The great distance traveled and the short time allotted to the journey has, necessarily, made the work accomplished far more cursory and imperfect than I could have desired.

From Omaha, Nebr., we proceeded west over the Union Pacific Railroad to Rock Creek Station, and thence by ambulance through Forts Fetterman and McKinney to our rendezvous on Tongue River, Wyoming, where the reconnaissance proper began. From this point the route continued into the Big Horn Mountains, by the side of Tongue River

Cañon and the North Fork to the top of the range; along the ridge to Black Cañon and down to the site of old Fort C. F. Smith; along the base of Pryor Mountains to the gap; over to Clark's Fork of the Yellowstone and up this to the mouth of the Clark's Fork Cañon; through the Clark's Fork Mountains to the National Park and out by way of Henry's Lake and the Camas Meadows to Camas Station, Idaho. This portion of the journey, some 500 miles long, passing over many very interesting and, hitherto, but little known regions, was made on horseback, between August 4 and September 2, after which we returned through Ogden, Utah, and home by rail.

The country included in the whole route traversed may, for convenience, be considered under its three most obvious natural divisions, viz, alluvial plains, sand-wastes or Bad Lands, and mountain country, each distinct in soil, climate, and botanical features.

THE ALLUVIAL PLAINS.

Under this head is included a vast extent of our western prairies east of the Rocky Mountains, until recently but little appreciated as an agricultural country, and regarded at least as only suited for pastoral purposes, but really valuable, and no doubt destined soon to occupy a place among our most productive lands.

The surface is comparatively even, smooth, and rolling. In early spring, when rain is abundant, the plains are beautiful; cleared of all rubbish by the fires, with fresh grass springing up, and a variety of early flowers, with pure air, and an unobstructed view, the landscape presents charms rarely equaled. The soil is deep and rich, possessing every quality necessary to productiveness, and, as shown by recent experience, needs only cultivation to make it productive and to bring about a complete revolution in both climate and flora. As compared with the earlier-settled States east, the climate is drier, especially in summer, and the total amount of rainfall is less. Detailed statistics on this point are as yet meager and unreliable, though it may be stated in general terms that, beginning at the Missouri River, with a fall of some 30 or 35 inches, the precipitation diminishes pretty uniformly towards the west to about 10 inches or less in the driest places, and again rises slightly near the base and under the influence of the mountains. The rainfall has increased of late years and promises a still greater improvement in the future; but even this amount compares favorably with that of many parts of Europe, as will be seen from the following table, quoted from Guyot, by Professor Aughey, in his Physical Geography of Nebraska:

Table of rainfall.

	Depth in inches.
British Islands	32
Western France	25
Eastern France	22
Sweden	21
Central and Northern Germany	20
Hungary	17
Eastern Russia, Kasson	14
Northeast Portugal	11
Madrid	10

Uninfluenced by cultivation, the flora of the plains is comparatively simple and meager, consisting, for the most part, of the hardier species peculiar to dry, exposed situations. But few plants common in the

Eastern States are found; density of fiber and a stunted development characterize most of the native kinds, the natural results of the numerous hardships and vicissitudes to which they are subjected; the leaves and stems of many, as, for example, the different species of astragalus, cinque-foil, sage, and anemone, are provided with a thick villous or hairy covering to protect them from sudden changes of temperature and to guard against the too rapid escape of precious moisture.

Plants with perennial stems are effectually destroyed and kept down by the fires which yearly sweep over this whole region in summer, often beginning as early as the 1st of July. The young shoots of trees, for example, could hardly escape more than a year or two, unless protected by some natural barrier; as when on an island, or in the crevices of rocks, or close along the margin of streams. Trees and shrubs are, therefore, seldom seen, except a straggling growth of mostly cottonwood, willows, or box-elder, in some such sheltered situations. Many of the late annuals are burned before ripening their seeds, and thus, eventually, become exterminated. The early annuals, or such as have annual stems, are the kinds most likely to survive, and hence the most numerous, but as these die down early, the surface is the earlier prepared for fires, which are sure to be started. Thus stripped of the taller grasses, sedges, shrubs and trees, the denuded surface is deprived of its natural shelter and exposed to the parching sun of the hottest part of summer and the upheaval of frost in winter.

Such plants only as can stand this sort of treatment are found on the plains, and it is no wonder their number is comparatively small or their characters peculiar. Prominent among the more useful of these is the Buffalo grass (*Buchloa dactyloides*, Engl.), the prevailing species covering the plateaus.

It is often associated with *Munroa squarrosa*, Torr., having some resemblance to it, but of very inferior quality. The former bears the fertile and sterile flowers on separate stems of the same plant, the seeds being close to the ground and the male flowers four or five inches above it. *Eriocoma cuspidata*, Nutt., and several species of *Grama** are also common on the high grounds. In the bottoms and along streams the porcupine grass (*Stipa comata*), beard grass (*Andropogon furcatus* and *scoparius*), wild rye (*Elemus Canadensis*), *Hordeum pratense* and *jubatum*, *Phragmites communis*, and *Spartina cynosuroides* are the prevailing species. But it is needless to dwell upon what the plains were or are, for with the recent influx of emigration, the opening of railroads, and the crowding of settlers upon the eastern and western borders, the old conditions are rapidly passing away and a new and improved state of things is taking place. The plains as they were a few years ago, with their countless herds of buffalo, antelope, deer, and wolves, with their long stretches without wood and water, dry and parched in summer, and black with ashes in the fall, are almost a thing of the past. With the advance of settlements, the suppression of prairie fires, and the breaking up of the surface with the plow, there has been a modification of the climate, increased production of the soil, and an entire revolution in the forms of plant life.

*The term *Grama*, now applied to the various species of *Boutelona* in our Southwest, evidently comes from Spain. It is there applied to what we know here as Bermuda or scutah grass (*Cynodon dactylon*, Pursh.), introduced among us from Southern Europe, and also found now widely distributed over the warmer parts of the globe. *Gramma* is incorrect, and *grass*, as *a suffix*, is *superfluous*. The use of the name was evidently suggested here by the one-sided arrangement of the spikelets, so like that in *Cynodon dactylon.*—J. T. ROTHROCK.

Traveling west from Omaha through Nebraska, one may notice the wonderful change that has taken place in the flora of the country in recent times. From the reports of Lewis and Clarke, in 1804, and Frémont, in 1842, the buffalo grass was almost the only kind along the Missouri River, and for a long time afterwards was the principal pasturage depended upon by freighters across the plains. Now it has receded nearly to the boundary of Wyoming, and is rapidly disappearing from the State. Grasses, sedges, and weeds indigenous to a more moist climate have taken its place, and trees are increasing into groves and forests in the vacant spaces. The oak, hickory, walnut, elm, and other valuable species, already flourish in the eastern part of the State, and would do well farther west if given a chance, but the quick-growing, though comparatively valueless, catalpa, cottonwood, and box-elder seem to be almost the only kinds selected for planting.

Fields of wheat and corn are now found growing on the bluffs two hundred miles west of the Missouri, and trees and gardens are cultivated at Sidney, where, in 1866, there was little vegetation except the buffalo grass. These wonderful improvements in the production of the soil are not confined to Nebraska alone, but extend along the whole frontier from Canada to the Gulf of Mexico. Any one familiar with the appearance of Kansas, Indian Territory, and Texas, as they were fifteen or twenty years ago, and are now, will recognize the same change going on there that is noticed here. From east to west, step by step, with a progress exactly proportionate to the advance of settlements, the change has been wrought. Native grasses and weeds have disappeared from the treeless monotonous plain, and fruitful fields, shady groves, and a multitude of vegetable farms have appeared in their stead.

Simultaneously with the occupation of the land by the agriculturist, and evidently in some way dependent upon it, there has appeared a favorable modification in the climate, with increase in the amount and a more equable distribution of the rainfall. The fact of a positive increase in the average annual amount of rain over the greater portion of our western plains, in recent years, is generally admitted, but the causes that have brought it about, and the probable permanency of the change, is a subject of some interest, and one on which various opinions prevail. The assumption that there are great cycles of increase and decrease in the rain-fall of a given region is unsupported by evidence and improbable. There are no known secular or cosmical conditions now existing, independent of the agency of man, which could have any influence in the production of this phenomenon. If there are such, they have yet to be discovered and pointed out. There are abundant indications of a more moist climate in former ages, when the plains were lower and bodies of water larger and more numerous; when, for example, Salt Lake stood at its old water marks on the mountain sides, hundreds of feet above its present level. But these conditions have passed away and the opposite tendency now prevails. We need, I think, go no farther than to observe the application of a few simple mechanical principles in connection with the cultivation of the land itself to find the influences which are at work to modify the climate and favor an increase of rain. The average annual amount of aqueous vapor rising into the atmosphere to form clouds over the oceans, lakes, and rivers of the globe is probably nearly constant, or, if increasing or decreasing, the change must be slow and gradual, through a long series of years.

Over the land, on the contrary, the quantity varies with the absorptive power of the surface. The more extended the absorbing surface the greater the evaporation, and, consequently, the greater the amount of cloud moisture available for precipitation. The effect of plowing up extensive tracts of the prairie has been to produce a new absorbing surface over wide adjoining areas, upon which the water is received and retained, economized, and utilized in the locality where it falls. The soil of Nebraska, Kansas, Texas, and Colorado is an alluvial deposit capable of packing to a great hardness, and tramped down by vast herds of wild animals and baked in the sun, the surface became as if covered by a layer of adobes and shed water like a brick pavement. It mattered but little whether ten, twenty, or thirty inches of rain fell in the year; it was not absorbed, but ran off in the ravines, creeks, and rivers, to the ocean from whence it came. The little remaining on the surface, being unprotected by the shade of clouds or trees or tall grass, was quickly dissipated and blown away; and in the hot months, when the atmospheric moisture fell far below its saturating point, all rain clouds were absorbed, and the sun's rays penetrated with unobstructed intensity, to dry up the sparse vegetation and prepare it for the prairie fire which inevitably followed. But with the tilling of the soil all this was changed. The compact surface once broken up with the plough, the rainfall was no longer wasted, but remained in the soil, to be given back to the air at the place where it fell, to moisten the leaves of plants, to furnish cloud shade, to favor the growth of trees and tall grasses, and thus to increase the total amount of evaporation and precipitation. From experiments made by Professor Aughey, as to the relative absorptive power of unbroken prairie and cultivated land, it appears that on equal areas the latter takes up ten or twelve times as much moisture as the former.

With a like amount of rain, ten times as much is retained and becomes available for saturating the soil and the atmosphere in the one case as in the other. Whatever other causes there may be tending to produce a more moist climate on the plains, cultivation of the soil is, certainly, one cause. That it is the principal, if not the only one, may reasonably be inferred from the fact that the improvement in climate has advanced step by step with the progress of agriculture. Attempts at cultivation in isolated places beyond the settlements, as, for example, at the military posts at Harker and Yard, in 1867, at Larned and Dodge, in 1868 and 1869, and at Richardson, Texas, in 1870, were unsuccessful. Many failures and disappointments occurred to those who ventured too far beyond the main line, and were driven back by drought. But gradually, as new inroads were made each year into the uncultivated district, an increase of rain prepared the way for further advances the next. The case is similar at places where irrigation was practiced. As the area of cultivated lands extended from year to year, the necessity for irrigation became less and less, because there was a more moist atmosphere and more rain. Starting from the older settlements along the eastern frontier of the plains, where the climate was most favorable, and from the base of the mountains in Colorado and New Mexico, where irrigation was practicable, the two lines have advanced from the east on one side and from the west on the other, until now more than half that region, once regarded as a hopeless waste, is spanned with flourishing farms.

And now, since the *cause* of this improvement may be regarded as permanent, the *effects* will also be permanent, and the change will doubtless go on until at no distant day the entire alluvial plains will be covered with grain fields, orchards, and forests, while the adjoining sand-wastes and bad lands, under the influence of a more general distribution of moisture, will have advanced a step in the process of metamorphosis to the condition of alluvial soil, preparatory in their turn to cultivation.

There is nothing in the character of the so-called "bad lands" to entitle them to the designation of a true desert. The surface is composed for the most part of the somewhat variable constituents of disintegrated eruptive rock. In some places the sand is deep and the little rain that falls upon it soaks away beyond the roots of plants, and in others the alkaline ingredient is so much in excess as to be deleterious to their growth. The general aspect is that of a barren, desolate, and often broken country, with a loose, shifting surface and a very meager and scattering vegetation. The country along our route from Fort Fetterman to Powder River, from Pryor's Gap to the Clark's Fork Cañon, around Camas Station, and that between Ogden and Rock Creek, is much of this sort, interspersed with alluvial districts.

Most of the valleys of the Big Horn and Stinking Water, between Big Horn and Clark's Fork Mountains, is equally unpromising. As a whole, these regions present the appearance of being at an earlier stage in the process of development from their former eruptive or submerged state to that of arable lands, having, as yet, sustained but little, and in some places no vegetation to mingle with the mineral matter of the surface. With the present deficient rainfall, it may be a long time before the needed vegetable constituents will be added, in the process of growth and decay, to form a soil suitable for tillage, but this is gradually taking place, and even now the transformation from lava beds to fertile land may be seen in every stage of its progress.

The flora of the Bad Lands is more interesting as an example of the persistence and endurance of some forms of plant life, under the most unfavorable conditions, than from the number or variety of the species.

The following, sparsely scattered over the sandy alkaline plateaus, stunted, straggling, and repulsive in appearance, are fair representatives of the chief conspicuous forms:

Artemisia ana.

      tridentata.
      rigida.   "Sage Brush."
      biennis.

Eurotia lanata.   "White Sage."
Snoeda Torrezana.
Corispermum hyssopifolium.   "Bug Seed."
Sarcobatus vermiculatus.   "Chico," "Greasewood."
Bigloria graveolens.
Opuntia Missouriensis.   "Missouri Cactus."

Closer observation reveals the presence here and there of diminutive specimens of the grama and buffalo grass. The most interesting in the above list is the white sage (*Eurotia lanata*), which, though extremely stunted and unpromising in appearance, was eagerly sought after by our animals, and is said to be very nutritious and fattening. It is reported by Mr. Watson to impart an unpleasant flavor to the flesh of cattle fed on it, and also to be a remedy in intermittent fever, and I will add that all the sages have long had the same reputation in both respects. This plant is sometimes known as "Winter fat" in Colorado and New Mexico.

In contrast with the horribly smelling sage is the fragrant abronia (*Abronia fragrans*), specimens of which were found near Camas Station, Idaho. Its general appearance is similar to the abronias (*Umbellata* and *arenaria*) in cultivation, from California. The matchless fragrance of this plant will make it a valuable addition to gardens and greenhouses.

THE MOUNTAIN COUNTRY.

Ascending the Big Horn Range from Tongue River, August 2, the monotony of dry, dusty plains was at once exchanged for cool, refreshing mountain parks, with beautiful trees, luxuriant grasses, and brilliantly colored flowers, and everywhere resounding with the ripple of clear, cold waters. The difference of climate and botanical features between the mountains and plains is so great as to be almost totally distinct. The one depends upon rain, as it falls from time to time, for its supply of water; the other has, in addition, a system of natural irrigation, independent of rainfall. In one case the supply is irregular and often insufficient; in the other it is regular, abundant, and nearly the same each year. On the bare unsheltered plains, exposed to sun and wind, the moisture is quickly dissipated, and long seasons of drouth often follow, but on the mountains it is *held in store* by the frost, and given up as needed, in regular and constant quantities.

The reservoirs of supply are the great banks of snow that accumulate during a long winter on the mountain tops, and are distributed as they slowly melt throughout the summer, until snow falls again. The remains of snow-banks were numerous during August, at 9,000 feet and upwards, and in many places the piles are so large and deep as to last over from year to year. One in the Bear Tooth Range, August 18, covered a space some 20 miles long by 10 miles wide, where it has probably remained for centuries.

This melting snow is the source of thousands of little irrigating streams, trickling down the slopes, forming marshes and springs, and uniting into brooks and creeks and rivers as they descend to the plains.

Cool vapors settle down from it through the foliage of the mountain sides, until they mingle with the heated air that rises from below, and there the two climates and the two floras meet and pass into each other, on a more or less definite line, from 4,000 to 5,000 feet above the level of the sea, where the timber ends and the plains begin. The cool moist air of the mountains is favorable to rain, and showers are more frequent and regular than on the plains.

The winters are long and severe, and the summers correspondingly short, but wonderfully fruitful. The soil is rich and deep with the decay of a luxuriant growth of tall grasses and sedges and underbrush for hundreds of years. The flora offers a rich harvest to the botanist, and, unlike that of the plains, includes many species familiar in more eastern localities. Already at the foot-hills we meet with cedars, spruces, pines, and cottonwoods increasing into dense forests at 8,000 and 9,000 feet, surrounding the parks and extending up the slopes to timber line. In the lower altitudes the red cedar (*Juniperis virginiana*) is found in considerable quantity, of medium size, and the ground cedar (*J. sabina*, var. *procumbens*) lying as flat to the surface as a carpet, covered many open spaces on the hill-sides, for great distances. The Douglases spruce, so much prized in cultivation as a lawn ornament, is found here in all its beauty, though not so large and coarse as on the Pacific slope, seldom exceeding 150 feet, while there it is known to reach 350 feet. It forms a large part of the forest in the Big Horn Range, but is somewhat less abundant in the Clark's Fork Mountains, and becomes comparatively rare in the Yellowstone Park. Its botanical place has recently been fixed by Dr. Engleman, of Saint Louis, as *Pseudotsuga Douglasii*, Engl. It ranks among the largest and best American forest trees. The twisted branch pine (*Pinus contorta*), about 1 foot in diameter and from 40 to 60 feet high, is also a beautiful tree and increases in fre-

3 SII

quency towards the west, until, in the National Park, it forms by far the largest portion of the timber. The trunks are remarkably straight and smooth, but are not much prized for sawed lumber, as the boards are liable to warp. The inner surface of the bark of this species, in early summer, is highly prized as a delicacy by some persons, and hence the trees all along the trails and around camping places in the park are girdled and skinned by tourists to obtain the coveted morsel. An abundant gummy exudation covering the trunk and branches aids in the spread of forest fires and leads to its own destruction. The American Cembran pine (*Pinus flexillis*), distinguished for its slow growth, occurs less frequently. Small clusters were noticed on the higher elevations about Black Cañon, and scattering specimens on barren ridges at Pryor's Gap and Clark's Fork, 20 to 30 feet high. This tree is often called white pine, under the impression that it is identical with the white pine of the east, which it somewhat resembles, but the species are distinct, and it is crooked and knotty and very inferior to the latter.

The western yellow pine (*Pinus ponderosa*) a large and valuable tree for fuel and lumber, is comparatively rare in the Big Horn and Clark's Fork Mountains. The balsam poplar (*Populus balsamifera*) and the willow-leaved poplar (*P. angustifolia*) are met with in groves of considerable extent in moist places, where the smooth gray bark of the latter contrasts prettily with the dark-green foliage of the coniferæ. Cottonwood (*Populus monilifera*), and American aspen (*P. tremuloides*) are more rare, and no oak, walnut, or ash was seen in the mountains, though the latter is found on Tongue River, below the cañon. Along the streams and in moist places of the middle and lower altitudes, the following berries are abundant, and furnish a delicate food for the grizzly and other kinds of bears :

Prunus Virginiana. Choke cherry.
Ribes setosum. Prickly gooseberry.
   floridium. Black currant.
   aureum. Mo. currant.
   lacustra. Currant.
Shepherdia argentea. Buffalo berry.
   Canadensis. Bull berry.
Fragira Virginiana. Strawberry.

Tongue River Cañon and Black Cañon, in the Big Horn, Pryor's Gap, and many places along Clark's Fork Cañon, where these berries abound, are favorite resorts and good hunting places for bears.

Strawberries were very abundant from the mouth of Crandell Creek to the boundary of the park, August 16 to 20, and especially at the head of Clark's Fork, August 19.

The pasturage in the parks was excellent, and in fact all that could be desired. The open spaces are everywhere covered with a thick growth of the most nutritious grasses. The great number and good quality of the varieties is remarkable. The following were collected in a single locality, around one of our camps near the head of the North Fork of Tongue River, at 9,000 feet, August 5.

Aira Pespitosa. Hair bunch grass.
Atropis tennifolia.
Bromus Kalmii. }
   ciliatus. } Brome grass.
Festuca rubra. Fescue grass.
Hordeum pratense.
Poa cæsia, var. *strictior.* }
   purpurascens. } Meadow grass.

Phleum Alpinum. Alpine timothy.
Stipa viridula. Feather grass.
Triticum repens. Quick grass.

Many other kinds were found elsewhere and appear in the list. The proportion in which these grasses grow varies, but as a rule the bunch grasses prevail, and the better kinds, as fescue grass, meadow grass, alpine timothy, and beard grass (*Andropogon scoparius* and *furcatus*). As the season is later or earlier in proportion to the altitude, animals may find fresh green grass all through the month of August, by following up near the snow line. Elk and deer go up as soon as the snow melts to the cool air and fresh grass of the parks, where they spend the summer until driven back by the storms in the fall. The parks of these mountains offer pasturage for thousands of cattle in the middle and latter part of summer, when it is dried up or burned off on the plains, and there is no difficulty in the way of getting herds in or out from the first of July to the end of September.

The most striking characteristic which distinguishes this and many other parts of the Rocky Mountain system is its numerous and extensive parks.

No description can do justice to many of those in which our camps were pitched through the Big Horn and Clark's Fork Ranges. The mountains are not crowded together into rugged and inaccessible peaks, but spread out over a wide space, with extensive valleys and meadows between, from 7,000 to 9,000 feet high, which, once reached, readily communicate with each other. Sheltered by surrounding hills and forests, and supplied with every requisite for grazing purposes, they must sooner or later be utilized for the feeding of stock, especially in summer, when pasturage fails at other places.

The beautiful as well as the useful is to be met with here, and flowers, the most gay and delicate, are not wanting to lend their charms to these wild and unfrequented regions.

The meadows and hillsides were everywhere brilliant with blue, scarlet, yellow, and white, and almost every conceivable shade and combination of these colors. A single example will illustrate what was a subject of frequent remark in passing through the parks of the Big Horn Mountains.

The following showy species were common all along our route, and often might all be seen at one time in full bloom and fresh and brighter notwithstanding that it was the middle of August:

Lupinus argenteus. Bright blue.
Mertensia siberica. Deep indigo.
Gentiana serrata. Dark blue.
G. anifis. Dark blue.
Castelleia miniata. Scarlet.
C. linariaefolia. Scarlet.
Geranium Richardsonii. Deep red.
E. pilobium angustifolia. Bright red.
Troximon glaucum. Lemon yellow.
Eriogonum umbellatum. Yellow.
Phlox longiafolia, var. *brevifolia.* Milk white.

Around the melting snow banks were collected, in August, buttercups, daisies, forget-me-nots, ground phlox, larkspurs, and many other flowers in great profusion, and although the ground was often covered with frost in the morning, and sometimes *ice* formed in our water buckets, and the tender petals of these plants were crisp with the frozen dew, they did not seem to be injured by it, and looked as bright and fresh as ever in the hot sun that quickly followed.

All forms of vegetation in these mountains must be accustomed to grow and bloom in the frost, for it is rather the exception than the rule not to have it at night, even though the temperature may have been as high as 80° or 85° F. during the day. The phlox grows flat on the ground, and covers the hillsides in some places with its flowers white as the snow itself. It is very handsome, and will pay for the trouble of cultivation farther east; and so will several others, especially *Clematis Douglasii* and *Myosotis Sylvatica* (var. *Alpestris*), and *Lupinus argenteus*, which ornaments the way with its large blue racemes all through the mountains to the Continental Divide, where its place is taken by a still larger species, *L. ornatus.*

Calochortus Gunnisoni and *Zygadenus elegans* are very much superior to many plants we find in the gardens.

The root of *Carum Gairdneri*, found all through the park and along Henry's Fork, is reported by Brewer and Watson, in the Flora of California, to be an important article of food among the Indians of the Pacific coast. They are said to use this, and also *C. Kelloggii* and most of the species of *Cymopterus* and *Paucedanum*. It is probable that the "Camas meal" is made from one or all of these.

The specimen No. 63 in the list, if not the true "Camas," must be one of the plants used under that name.

The botanical specimens collected are numbered and deposited in the herbarium of the Harvard University, Cambridge, Mass. I am indebted to Mr. Sereno Watson, in charge, for valuable assistance in determining the species.

BOTANICAL LIST.

1. *Aquilegia flavescens*, Watson. Yellowstone Park. August.
2. *Anemone cylindrica*, Gray. Clark's Fork. August.
3. *Clematis Douglasii*, Hook. Big Horn Mountains. August 5.
4. *C. ligusticifolia*, Nutt. Big Horn and Clark's Fork. August.
5. *Delphinum Menziesii*, D. C. Parks Clark's Fork Mountains. August.
6. *D. exaltatum*, Ait. Yellowstone Park. August.
7. *D. occidentale*, Watson. Head of Clark's Fork. August.
8. *Ranunculus affinis*, R. Br. Around snow banks, Big Horn. August.
9. *Argemone hispida*, Gray. North Platte. July.
10. *Arabis Drummoudii*, Gray. Parks of the Big Horn. August.
11. *Sisymbrium canescens*, Nutt. Tongue River. August 3.
12. *Vesicularia alpina*, Nutt. Tongue River. August 3.
13. *Clemone intexrifolia*. T. and Z. Big Horn River, C. F. Smith. August.
14. *C. lutea*, Hook. Bad Lands, Camas Creek. September.
15. *Hypericum Canadense*, L. Clark's Fork Mountains. August.
16. *Arenaria congesta*, Nutt. Parks, Clark's Mountains. August.
17. *Cerastium alpinum*. var. *Behringianum*, Reg. Parks of the Big Horn. August.
18. *Geranium Richardsonii*, F. M. Parks Big Horn and Clark's Fork. August.
19. *Rhus toxicodendron*. Lr. Big Horn Mountains. August.
20. *Rhus*, Sumach. Banks Black Cañon. August.
21. *Vitis cordifolia*. Black Cañon. August; in fruit.
22. *Celastrus scandens*. L. Big Horn. August; in fruit.
23. *Negundo aceroides*. Very common below 5,000 feet.
24. *Polygala alba*, Nutt. Tongue River. Common.
25. *Astragalus Canadensis*, L. Big Horn and Clark's Fork Mountains.
26. *Caryocarpus*, Ker. Fort C. F. Smith; pods dry. August.
27. *A. triphyllus*, Pursh. Clark's Fork. August; out of bloom.
28. *Glycyrrhiza lepidota*, Nutt. Tongue River. Common.
29. *Lupinus argenteus*, Pursh. Parks Big Horn and Clark's Fork Mountains. August.
30. *L. cœspitosus*, Nutt. Yellowstone Park. August.
31. *L. ornatus*, Doug. Camas Creek, Idaho. August 31.
32. *Psoralea esculenta*, Pursh. Mouth Black Cañon.
33. *P. caudidus*, Michx. Clark's Fork.
34. *P. lanceolata*, Pursh. Camas Creek. September 2.

35. *Vicia Americana*, Musk. Tongue River. Common.
36. *Fragaria Virginiana*, Ehr. Clark's Fork Mountains. Common.
37. *Geum trefolium*, R. Brown. Park Big Horn Mountains. August 4.
38. *Potentilla dissecta*, Pursh. Parks Big Horn and Clark's Fork Mountains. August.
39. *P. fructicosa*, Linn. Common all through the parks.' August.
40. *P. Plattensis*, Nutt. Clark's Fork. August.
41. *Prunus Virginiana*,L. Tongue River, Pryor's Gap; berries ripe. August
42. *Rosa blanda*, Ait. Very common along streams everywhere.
43. *Rubus Nuthanus*, Moc. Crandell Creek. August 17.
44. *Spirola betulæfolia*, Pall. Head Clark's Fork. August 19.
45. *Ribes aureum*, Pursh. Big Horn, Clark's Fork Mountains.
46. *R. floridum*. L. Big Horn and Clark's Fork Mountains.
47. *Ribes lacustre*, Poir. Big Horn Mountains. August; in fruit.
48. *R. irriguum*, Dougl. Clark's Fork Mountains. August; ripe.
49. *R. setosum*, Doug. Big Horn Mountains.
50. *R. Viscosissimum*, Pursh. Yellowstone Park.
51. *Saxifraga nivalis*, L. Big Horn Mountains. August 5.
52. *Sedum stenopetalum*, Pursh. Big Horn Mountains. August.
53. *Epilobium angustifolium*. Linn. Big Horn Mountains. August.
54. *E. coloratum*, Muhl. Parks Big Horn. August 5.
55. *E. paniculatum*, Muhl. Bovis Creek. August 11.
56. *Guara parriflora*, Dougl. Big Horn. August.
57. *Gay ophytum diffusum*, T. and G. Crandell Creek. August.
58. *Œnothera breviflora*, Nutt. Yellowstone Park.
59. *Œ. pinnatifida*, Nutt. Dry ridges Big Horn and Clark's Mountains.
60. *Opintia Missouriensis*, D. C. Common on sand wastes everywhere.
61. *Mamellaria vivipara*, Ham. Sage Creek; rare.
62. *Bupleurum ranunculoides*, L. Big Horn Mountains. August 5.
63. *Carum Sairdoaeri*, Benth. and H. Parks Clark's Fork. August.
64. *Carnus stolonifera*. Tongue River and Big Horn Mountains.
65. *Linnæa borealis*, Leon. Shady places, Clark's Fork Mountains. August 19.
66. *Symphoricarpus occidentalis*, Brown. Along streams.
67. *S. vulgaris*, Michx. Big Horn Mountains.
68. *Galium boreale*, L. Clark's Fork Mountains. August 19.
69. *Valeriana edulis*, Nutt. Head of Clark's Fork. August 19.
70. *Liatris punctata*, Hook. Head of Clark's Fork. Common. August.
71. *Achillea millefolium*, L. Common through mountains. August.
72. *Ambrosia trifida*, L. Tongue River. Common.
73. *Anaphalis margaritacea*, Bueth. Tongue River.
74. *Arnica cordifolia*, Parks. Big Horn and Clark's Fork Mountains.
75. *Artemesia biennis*. Clark's Fork. Common.
76. *Artemisia Canadensis*, Michx. Clark's Fork.
77. *A. frigida*, Thilla. Clark's Fork. Common. August.
78. *A. tridentata*, Nutt. Very common on bad lands and elsewhere.
79. *Arnica Panyi*, Gray. Head of Clark's Fork. Common. August.
80. *Aster adscendens*, Lind. Yellowstone. August.
81. *A. conspicuus*, Lind. Yellowstone. August.
82. *A. multiflorus*, Ait. Clark's Fork. August.
83. *Byiloria Douglasii*, Gray. Common on bad lands. August.
84. *B. graneolens*, Gray. Crandell Creek. Common. August.
85. *Bahia integrifolia*, D. C. Head Clark's Fork. August 19.
86. *Chalnactis*, Doug. Upper Geyser Basin. August 26.
87. *Erignon salsuginosus*, Gray. Parks Big Horn. August.
88. *Echinacea angustifolia*, D. C. Big Horn River. August.
89. *Franseria Hookerania*, Nutt. Camas Creek, Idaho. September 2.
90. *Gaillardia aristata*, Pursh. Head Clark's Fork. August.
91. *Grindelia squarrosa*, Dun. Tongue River.
92. *Helianthus lenticularis*, Doug. Tongue River and Clark's Fork. August.
93. *Iva xanthiifolia*, Nutt. Yellowston-.
94. *Lactuca pulchella*, D. C. Clark's Fork Mountains. August 16.
95. *Lygodesmia juncea*, Don. Tongue River. Common.
96. *L. spinosa*, Nutt. Camas Creek. September 2.
97. *Mulgedium pulchella*, Nutt. Big Horn Mountains.
98. *Solidago rigida*, L. Big Horn and Clark's Fork. August.
99. *Tretradymia canescens*. D. C. Crandell Creek. August 17.
100. *Troximon aurantiacum*, Hook. Head Clark's Fork. August 19.
101. *T. glaucum*, Nutt. Big Horn Mountains. August 5.
102. *Xanthium strumarium*, L. Tongue River and Clark's Fork.
103. *Campanula rotundifolia*, L. Parks Big Horn and Clark's Fork Mountains. August.

104. *Aistostaphylos Hva-ursi*, Sprey. Big Horn Mountains. In fruit.
105. *Plantago pusilla*, Nutt. Clark's Fork and Big Horn.
106. *Pholipata Ludviciana*. Big Horn River. August.
107. *Castillea miniata*, Dong. Parks Big Horn and Clark's Fork Mountains. August.
108. *C. linariœolia*, Bueth. Head of Clark's Fork. August 19.
109. *C. sessiliflora*, Pursh. Yellowstone.
110. *Mimulus luteus*, Linn. Wet places, Big Horn and Clark's Fork Mountains. August.
111. *Pentotamon confertus*, Dong., var. *caruleo purpurascens*. Yellowstone and Clark's Fork Mountains.
112. *P. sccundiflorus*, Bueth. Yellowstone. August.
113. *Menthal Canadensis* L. Shady places, Big Horn and Clark's Fork Mountains.
114. *Lycopus sinuostus*, Bueth. Clark's Fork Mountains. August.
115. *Monarda fistulosa*, L. Very common. Tongue River, &c.
116. *Lithospernum angustifolium*, Michx. Big Horn, &c.
117. *L. canescens*, Lehm. Big Horn River. Common.
118. *Mertensia sibirica*, Don. Along streams, Big Horn and Clark's Fork Mountains.
119. *Myosatis sylvatica*, Hoff., var. *alpestris*, Koch. Around snow-banks, Big Horn Mountains. August.
120. *Phlox longifolia*, Nutt., var. *brevifolia*, Gr. Very common around snow-banks and on hillsides. August.
121. *Gentiana affinis*, Gris. Parks Big Horn and Clark's Fork Mountains. August.
122. *G. serrata*, Linn. Parks Big Horn and Clark's Fork Mountains. August.
123. *G. detonsa*, Fries. Yellowstone Park. August.
124. *Severtia perennis*, L. Yellowstone. August.
125. *Apocynum carmabinum*, L. Tongue River.
126. *A. androsœmifoluim*, L. Clark's Fork.
127. *Asclepias Corruti*, Dic. Fort C. F. Smith. August; in fruit.
128. *Fraxinus Americana*, L. Tongue River, below cañon.
129. *Abronia fragrans*, Nutt. Camas Creek, Idaho. September 2.
130. *Oxybaphus hirsutus*, Hook. Camas Creek. September 2.
131. *Chenopodium album*, L. Tongue River and Clark's Fork.
132. *Eurotia lanata*, Maj. Pryor's Gap to Clark's Fork Mountains. Common.
133. *Corispermum hyssopifolium*, L. Bad Lands, Clark's Fork.
134. *Obione conferlifolia*, Torr. Pryor Mountains. Common.
135. *Sarcobatus vermiculatus*, Torr. Common on bad lands.
136. *Erigonum cernuum*, Nutt. Camas Creek. September 2.
137. *E. microthecum*, Nutt. Camas Creek. September 2.
138. *E. ovalifolium*, Nutt. Pryor's Gap, on rocks. August 12.
139. *E. umbellatum*, Torr. Parks of Big Horn Mountains. August 15.
140. *Polygonum ariculare*, L. Tongue River. Common.
141. *P. bistorta*, L. Park Clark Fork Mountains. August 19.
142. *P. ariculare*, var. *erectum*, L. Tongue River.
143. *P. dumetorum*. Pryor's Creek. August.
144. *Rumex paucifolius*, Nutt. Parks Big Horn Mountains. August.
145. *Shepherdia argentia*, Nutt. Big Horn; rare. August; in fruit.
146. *S. Canadensis*, Nutt. Tongue River. August; in fruit.
147. *Euphœbia marginata*, Pursh. Big Horn plateaus.
148. *E. dictyosperma*, F. M. Yellowstone.
149. *Humulus lupulus*, L. Tongue River, Bovais Creek.
150. *Helmus Americana*. Tongue River.
151. *Belula occidentales*, Hook. Tongue River.
152. *Populus angulata*, Ait. Tongue River.
153. *P. angustifolia*, James. Big Horn Mountains and Tongue River. Common.
154. *P. balsamifera*, L. Tongue River, Big Horn and Clark's Fork Mountains. Common.
155. *P. monilifera*, Ait. Common along streams.
156. *P. tremuloides*, Michx. Big Horn Mountains.
157. *Salix cordata*, Muhl. Common along streams.
158. *S. longifolia*, Muhl. Along streams, Big Horn and Clark's Fork.
159. *S. nigra*, Maich. Among streams, &c., Big Horn and Clark's Fork Mountains.
160. *Juniperus communis*, L. Big Horn Mountains. Rare.
161. *J. Sabina*, var. *procumbens*, Pursh. Foot-hills Big Horn. Common.
162. *J. Virginiana*, L. Big Horn Mountains and Camas Creek.
163. *Pinus contorta*, Dougl. Big Horn, Clark's Fork Mountains, and Yellowstone Park.
164. *P. flexillis*, James. Big Horn and Clark's Fork Mountains.
165. *P. ponderosa*, Dougl. Big Horn and Clark's Fork Mountains. Not common.
166. *Pseudotsuga Douglasii*, Engl. The prevalent tree, Big Horn Mountains.
167. *Typha latifolia*, L. Bovais and Pryor Creeks.
168. *Habenaria hypebrorea*, Gray. Clark's Fork Mountains. August.

169. *Smilax herbacea*, L. Bovais Creek.
170. *Alium breristylum*, Watson. Big Horn Mountains. August.
171. *A. reticulatum*, Fras. Big Horn and Clark's Fork Mountains. Common.
172. *Calochortus Gunnisoni*, Watson. Head Clark's Fork. August 19.
173. *Spiranthes Romanzofiana*, Cham. Yellowstone Park.
174. *Yucca angustifolia*, Pursh. Old Fort C. F. Smith. Common.
175. *Zygadenus elegans*, Pursh. Park Clark's Fork Mountains. August.
176. *Juncus Xipheoides*, Meg. Yellowstone Park. August.
177. *Carex filifolia*, Nutt. Tongue River and Big Horn Mountains. Common.
178. *Agrostes scabra*, Willd. Yellowstone Park. August.
179. *Aira cæspitosa*, Linn. Parks Big Horn Mountains. August.
180. *Andropogon furcatus*, Muhl. Tongue River. August.
181. *A. scoparius*, Michx. Tongue River. August. Common.
182. *Atropis tenuifolia*, Thurber. Parks Big Horn Mountains.
183. *Bontelona curtipendula*, Gr. Tongue River.
184. *Bromus Kalmii*, Gray. Parks Big Horn Mountains. August.
185. *B. ciliatus*, Linn. Parks Big Horn Mountains. August.
186. *Buchlœ dactyloides*, Engl. Common grass of the prairie.
187. *Calamagrostis longifolia*, Hook. Yellowstone.
188. *Elymus Canadensis*, Braun. Along streams Big Horn and Clark's Fork Mountains.
189. *E. sitanion*, Shult. Tongue River. August.
190. *Erioconia cuspidata*, Nutt. Tongue River and Big Horn.
191. *Epiophorum polystachyon*. Yellowstone Park. August.
192. *Festuca rubra*, L. Parks Big Horn Mountains. August.
193. *Hordeum pratense*, Huds. Park Big Horn Mountains. August.
194. *H. jubatum*, L. Clark's Fork Mountains. August.
195. *Lepturus paniculatus*, Nutt. Big Horn and Clark's Fork Mountains.
196. *Melica bulbosa*, Sey. Yellowstone Park.
197. *Munroa squarrosa*, Torr. With buffalo grass, prairies.
198. *Phragmites communis*, Linn. Mouth Clark's Ford Cañon. August.
199. *Phlaris arundinaceæ*, L. Tongue River. August.
200. *Poa andina*, Nutt. Yellowstone Park. August.
201. *P. cæsia*, Smith, var. *Strictor*, Gray. Parks Big Horn. August.
202. *P. tenuifolia*, Nutt. Tongue River. August.
203. *P. purpurascens*, Vasey. Parks Big Horn Mountains. August.
204. *Phleum alpinum*, L. Parks Big Horn Mountains. August.
205. *Stipa comata*, Trim. Tongue River, &c. Common.
206. *S. Spartea*, Trim. Tongue River. August.
207. *S. viridula*, Trim. Parks Big Horn Mountains. August.
208. *Spartina cynosuroides*, Willd. Pryor Creek. Common.
209. *Sporobolus airoides*, Torr. Yellowstone. August.
210. *Triticum repens*, L. Park of the Big Horn and Clark's Fork Mountains.
211. *Triticum violaceum*, How. Clark's Fork Mountains.
212. *Vilfa cuspidata*, Torr. Big Horn, Clark's Fork Mountains.
213. *Berberis aquifolia*, Pursh. Clark's Fork Mountains. August; ripe berries.
214. *Subulonia aquatica*, L. Yellowstone Lake. August.
215. *Arnica Parrgi*, Gray. Clark's Fork Mountains. August 19.

Very respectfully, your obedient servant,

W. H. FORWOOD,
Surgeon, U. S. Army.

To the ADJUTANT-GENERAL,
Military Division of the Missouri.